THE DO IT YOURSELF GUIDE TO DIVORCE IN COLORADO

~Get In ~ Get Out ~ Get Over It

Teddi Ann

ISBN: 978-0-57862222-4

Any references to historical events, real people, or real places are used fictitiously. Names, characters, and places are products of the author's imagination.

Front cover image by Chris Hunter

Printed by Kindle Direct Publishing

First printing edition 2020.

www.UnifiedDivorce.org

www.DivorceInColorado.com

INTRODUCTION

Are You Ready to Divorce?
Where Do You Start?
What Do You Do Now!?

At this moment, that feels like you failed your family, your marriage, and the future you planned, remember life happens. The future holds answers and rewards you cannot yet imagine.

Remember, the *legal* Divorce is meant to be a brief 91-day process in Colorado. To separate the emotional experience from the legal procedure is to understand the Court only cares about the words and numbers and what seems fair and equitable.

Through this Do It Yourself (DIY) Guide to Divorce In Colorado, you will learn how to divorce successfully!

The Successful Divorce in Colorado is:

- Knowing How & What to Expect Before, During & After Your Divorce
- Understanding Effective Divorce Communication Through Successful Talk Tactics
- Gathering Information & Completing the Disclosure Process
- Drafting Your Financial Agreements Accurately
- Determining the Best Division of Your Debt & Assets
- Drafting Clear & Concise Agreements
- Moving On to Your New Life

Approximately 7 out of 10 couples are choosing a Do It Yourself Divorce in Colorado. People are too quick to think this process of Divorce is just filling out papers. They have a misconception that not hiring attorneys means they won't fight about anything. Failing to have proper legal advice before signing your documents can mean many more years of fighting if you fail to Divorce right the first time.

If you find yourself stuck, confused, or unclear about what to do, know that we offer complimentary consultations and unbundled services at DivorceInColorado & UnifiedDivorce. We can help with specific issues you may have or represent you and do the work for you.

Now let's ~Get In!

HOW & WHAT TO EXPECT BEFORE, DURING & AFTER YOUR DIVORCE

Expectations are huge, aren't they?

You expected to be married forever. You assumed that you would reap the benefits of your successes and be able to share your failures with your one and only - your person.

You expected that if you had children, you'd be there for everything in their life!

How? How do you now face life after a broken marriage? How do you leave with half or less and start over? How will "equal parenting time" now be half-time or less, or maybe all of it... all alone?

If you're thinking about divorce, make sure you thought of all the possible ways to repair your marriage first – and TRY ALL OF THEM!!!

Don't walk out that door or let her walk away if there is even a small chance of saving your marriage.

Here are some Expectations to consider when you decide to divorce.

EXPECTATION #1 DIVORCE IS A FINAL OPTION – NOT THE FIRST. YOU SHOULD ONLY GET DIVORCED IF YOU'VE TRIED EVERYTHING TO SAVE YOUR MARRIAGE

In this world of "me," society of change, and complicated lifestyles, people seem quick to blame the marriage or the one they've loved as the reason for the pain and issues.

There are often many stresses and symptoms that can be identified and handled before considering divorce.

Here are some ideas couples try before choosing divorce or saving their marriage.

- Marriage Counseling
- Rehab
- Financial Counseling
- Anger Management classes
- Diet & Nutrition planning
- Communication Workshops
- Intimacy Retreats
- Parenting Support Groups
- Implementing ALONE -time and date nights into weekly schedules
- Taking a vacation together far away from every distraction

When clients are considering divorce, but not yet ready to end their marriage, we explore this list of other problems and try to set up a 90-day process to figure it out. Whether through counseling, participating in the ideas above, or taking time in solitude, do not tread lightly into divorce.

Once you believe you tried everything or your spouse is no longer willing to try anything, Get Out! You can't make someone love you. You shouldn't stay in a relationship that makes you miserable or even unhappy any longer- knowing you've tried everything.

Take the time to make sure your spouse or the marriage is the issue and not any of the life distractions and irritations we experience. Be confident there is not an obstacle you can't overcome.

EXPECTATION #2
TAKE YOUR TIME. EXPECT YOUR DIVORCE TO BE A MARATHON - NOT A SPRINT.

Too often, there is a hostile argument, and one or the other will go to the courthouse and file the divorce on their own - having no clue what they are doing or what they just started – but just wanting the pain to end.

The first mile through a divorce is determining what you should file and when.

Ask yourself these questions.

- Do you have a timeline and have to be divorced as soon as possible?
- Can you file one Petition together, or will someone need to force the situation?
- How complex are the debts and assets you need to divide?

- What information do you need that you don't have?
- If you are parents, do you have an interim plan for the kids and parenting?
- Are both people going to do as they need in a reasonable amount of time?
- On a scale of 1-10, how likely are you to work together through the process?

Each state has a different timeline between the date you give the State notice that you want to divorce and when the State will grant the divorce legally. In Colorado, this process is a minimum of 91 days.

The *Petition* is the name of the document that begins the divorce, and the *Decree* is the document the Court signs legally granting your divorce at the end.

In traditional, contested divorces, one person files for divorce, and the other has 21 days to respond to the Petition by filing a "Response" and paying more fees to the court to begin the court process.

In uncontested and often with *pro se* divorces, meaning one or both parties represent themselves, the parties may file the Petition together, eliminating the need to file a Response or pay additional fees.

If your assets and debts are complicated, such as:

- An inheritance or family trusts
- Complex Debt
- Self-Employment or Business Ownership

Then you may want to delay filing the Petition for Dissolution until you have more information. Gathering information may take longer than the typical court deadlines consider.

Instead of filing your Petition for Dissolution of Marriage immediately, you can wait. You can exchange your financial information, draft your Agreements, and then file everything at once. Then wait for the 91 days to pass and your divorce to be final.

By not filing the Petition right away, you stay out of Court. Once someone files the Petition, there will be a Case Management Order, meetings set with a Court Facilitator, and deadlines and timelines forced upon you from day one. Filing your Petition for Dissolution sooner than later can add unnecessary stress for many couples.

Regardless of who knows what, or has what documents, you need time to gather your statements, account information, and asset values. Doing so before filing the Petition may be easier during this difficult time. Others find the court deadlines and pressure is helpful, so filing sooner to have the help of the Court to keep things moving may be the right choice for you.

EXPECTATION #3
EXPECT TO SHARE ALL INFORMATION

You can't hide accounts, assets, or things you don't think are marital property during a divorce. Make sure the other knows everything you have and its value before deciding who gets what. Understand that just because you disclose it, does not automatically mean you only keep half, but we'll discuss that later.

A married couple has a **"fiduciary responsibility"** to one another.

A "Fiduciary Relationship" is a relationship in which one party places special trust, confidence, and reliance on and is influenced by another who has a fiduciary duty to act for the benefit of the party. ~Merriam's Webster Dictionary.

Know that sharing all your information is key to a successful divorce. Failing to disclose information could lead to your divorce settlement being reopened and possibly changed years later! It's not worth it.

Better to share the information and negotiate what happens with the property or debt later than try to keep any secrets from one another during the divorce.

EXPECTATION #4
YOUR CHILDREN ARE THE PRIORITY

In addition to your responsibility to be open and honest with one another, you have an exceptional duty to your children. Parenting changes but does not stop with divorce. If children are involved, you need to have a plan for them.

Whether you file the Petition immediately or wait until you agree on all issues, know who is staying in the home. You may plan to live together until the divorce is final. If you're going to remain in the house together, start arranging separate parenting time to be with the kids. Also, decide a plan to leave if things become heated while you continue to live in the same home during the divorce.

If you are physically separating before the divorce is final, sit down and try to figure out how you will pay expenses for both households. The more you can keep things as they are until you have contractual agreements, the better.

Also, plan a parenting schedule for the next 90 days. It doesn't have to be the permanent parenting plan you'll have after divorce, but you need to understand the logistics from parents' work and travel schedules to the children's events and how to start trying to maneuver your family from 2 separate homes.

Consider how difficult it would be for you to move houses every few days. Try and avoid this for your kids in this time of transition. Think about dinner and after school events instead of sudden back and forth overnights. Think about their ages, their activities, and social life, and what you can do to make this transition easier for them.

The more consistent and routine you can keep the children's lives, the less stressful the divorce will be for everyone.

EXPECTATION #5
WHEN IT SEEMS YOU HAVE NOTHING LEFT – KEEP YOUR INTEGRITY

Regardless of why you decide to divorce - lies, infidelity, emotional absence, to be honest through the divorce process will save you money and time and help you divorce in a less contentious way. Honesty and clear communication can help to avoid emotional harm.

No matter how mad you may be, remember the divorce is a legal process first. "*Words and Numbers*" - keep a clear head and remember, you got into this marriage together, and it's best for everyone if you can work together to get out of the marriage as well.

In addition to being honest with your spouse, you must also be honest with yourself. Sometimes couples wanting to work together through their divorce just can't.

Divorce is emotional.

There may be fear or power issues within the relationship.

The sooner you figure out if you can cooperate or not, the better. Be honest.

EXPECTATION #6
YOU'RE GOING TO NEED HELP – GET IT!

Expect to need help and ask for it when you do.

When you cannot communicate, trust, or otherwise work through the divorce together, consider counseling – either a family therapist for all of you or individual counseling if you need help in different ways.

When you have questions about budgets, your investment accounts, or possible tax issues, meet with a financial advisor, CPA, or tax advisor.

If you can't decide what the home is worth or if someone should keep it, or better to sell, call a real estate agent – or two – and figure out a reasonable price or what if keeping or selling is best.

When you are ready to draft your legal documents, meet with an attorney. Also, please do not confuse a mediator with an attorney. Mediators are neutral parties unable to give anyone legal advice, often preparing agreements that can be flipped quickly by most litigators if not drafted properly.

If you need help drafting or negotiating the details of your agreements, go to the lawyers who end up in court litigating or fixing shitty mediation and *pro se* agreements – before you sign anything -not after the damage is done.

Know that many attorneys, offer complimentary consultations and unbundled services, meaning you can hire an attorney only to review and comment on the Agreements you draft after reading this. They don't have to represent you in court or file a bunch of documents you don't need. Just pay for an hour or two of advice to save yourself hours and many dollars if you do not do it right the first time.

The more we can trust to turn towards one another instead of away, the better off we are.

As difficult as divorce is, remember there was a time that the one you are leaving or who is walking away was the one you counted on most.

When you take the time to leave with grace, trust that there may still be a future and a moment when you need one another.

Do not do this alone. Regardless of the professional help you may need, you will need family and friends and the support of others to help. Divorce is temporary, and although it doesn't seem so, a very brief moment of your life.

There are on-line communities, social support groups, and other parents or professionals you know that are also going through or have experienced divorce too. Reach out when you need help and support.

Now that we've discussed some of the expectations to have when divorcing, let's discuss effective communication. Knowing how to speak to one another is so crucial for a successful divorce.

EFFECTIVE DIVORCE COMMUNICATION THROUGH SIMPLE TALK TACTICS

Knowing how to speak to one another in this challenging time can be the difference between a successful divorce and one that continues for years and years later.

Talk Tactics are simple and easy concepts to keep your communication open and honest while protecting you and your emotions through the Divorce.

Follow these Talk Tactics to help you through your Divorce successfully.

- ✓ Mean what you say and don't be mean
- ✓ Listen more than you talk
- ✓ Say only what is necessary and relevant
- ✓ Leave the past behind you and stay present
- ✓ Never react always respond
- ✓ Keep the end in mind from the very beginning

TALK TACTIC #1
ANYTHING YOU SAY MAY BE EVERYTHING.

Speak with integrity, equanimity, and honesty.

Integrity - keep it honest and upright. Have conversations about what matters and is essential without yelling. Don't engage in fighting - walk away and focus on the fix, not the fight.

You do not have to demean the other person to make your point.

Saying it louder doesn't make what you say more accurate or true.

Lying now won't make what you said true later and will absolutely diminish trust in an already stressful situation.

Equanimity may be the best skill you can learn and practice.

Equanimity is the evenness of mind,
especially under stress.

Be mindful of what you are saying and doing. Relax and know when and how to experience emotion separate from specific conversations about your divorce.

To communicate successfully with integrity and patience through divorce, try these tactics:

Choose an appropriate time for both people to talk.

Limit the subject matter so as not to overwhelm either of you during a single conversation.

Do not react - respond. Take time to listen, to pause, and then answer. If you must respond to something that has you heated or upset; it's OK to say, "let me think about that for a bit before I answer you."

Always keep in mind that once you speak it, you can't take it back. Be careful with your words during Divorce.

TALK TACTIC #2
LISTEN!

To listen is to understand. To understand is the most crucial part of negotiating your Divorce successfully.

So many of us jump in to talk, to make our point, to be heard!

When we practice equanimity, listening becomes much easier. Listening is often more important than speaking.

Know what the issue is, understand the fears involved, and take time to hear what may be significant to your spouse before sharing what is important to you.

TALK TACTIC #3
LIMIT COMMUNICATION AND CREATE HEALTHY BOUNDARIES.

Limiting communication sounds counter-intuitive, doesn't it? Shouldn't we talk every day and work this out?

How are we going to resolve anything if we limit communication? What are the boundaries?

You are entering a world where the end game or goal is most often limited contact and communication.

You are SEPARATING!!

Here are some ways to limit communication during Divorce.

Don't post to each other's social media accounts - stop engaging altogether!

If the text you think you want to send is more than five words, then either pick up the phone and call or send an email. Limit text messages to 5 words or less.

Texting, Calling, E-mailing after drinking, or doing drugs is a bad idea.

The communication window should be between 9-9 - that is it, and not while someone is at work or with the kids.

You do not talk about anything related to your Divorce when your kids are there.

Don't blindside each other. Set a date, time, and agenda of talking points and don't overdo it. Limit conversations to 1 or 2 issues at a time.

Only communicate once a week unless necessary.

By limiting the amount of time you spend together or talk, you create space and pause that allows for a personal perspective.

The absence often creates more respect for one another and lessens the emotional drama.

By limiting text and email communication, you have to practice listening. Remember, you will most likely still have to co-parent or manage social situations together.

Text and Email communication is almost always reaction communication. You can hide behind the screen, not realize the effects of what you type and possibly regret all of it in 10 minutes- or worse.

Remember, anything you email or text or put on social media is now recorded forever and may haunt you in litigation later. Don't do it.

Also, don't doubt that everyone has a weak moment or minute of "crazy" during a divorce. Just don't let it show in your communication with your soon to be *former* spouse.

By limiting text and email communication, you are also sending the signal and teaching your soon to be Ex that you are not always available. By creating the boundary of schedules and expectations, you are setting clear messages about when you are ready to talk and, therefore, making communication so much more effective.

Leave the past behind you and stay present. Get Over it! Your yesterday is behind you - leave it there. Sure, there should be some future therapy to help you figure out what happened and how to NOT re-do the unfortunate past, but this is a separate exercise from negotiating and resolving your Divorce.

Limiting Communication and Creating Boundaries is an absolute MUST for effective communication during your Divorce.

TALK TACTIC # 4
MAKE RESOLUTION THE REALITY

People always want someone to blame. People know what's behind them and often fear the future in a way that makes constantly talking about the past easier.

When couples stay in the past, it is difficult to talk about the future. When the past consumes you or your spouse, the focus is on the problems instead of all the solutions.

You can't divide the anger or regrets - you'll each have to deal with that separately from the legal contract. No one is getting punished for "bad behavior" during the marriage through your Divorce, so stop talking about it.

Let go of the past. Talk about today and what is ahead of you after your successful Divorce. Focus on the fix - not the fight.

Concentrating on Resolution may sound like this:

"Is what you're saying relevant to what we are discussing right now?"

"Can we talk about that another time, after we finish this conversation about...."

If you catch yourself going backward, acknowledge it, apologize, and refocus. Focus on making each communication effective in realizing the goal of getting through your divorce successfully.

Directed and focused communication is more positive, unloaded, less emotional dialogue. Remember, this process is to figure out the numbers involved and translate the division into the words that become your contract.

TALK TACTIC #5
NEVER REACT ALWAYS RESPOND

To react is to shoot from the hip, run your mouth before you know what you are saying, and let everything stem from emotion rather than any common sense or place of mindful reality.

To respond is to read or hear what is said to you, pause to understand and process, and then continue the conversation. If your spouse sends a text, you can read it right away, but don't text back immediately. When you read an email, don't start typing instantly.

It's fine to respond if the message is "running 10 mins late." or something not relevant to your relationship or the Divorce.

Take time and be mindful of all your communication. Respond, do not react.

TALK TACTIC #6
KEEP THE END IN MIND FROM THE VERY BEGINNING.

You will get through this regardless if you make it easy or difficult. This Guide will help you get through this process as fast as possible while being thorough and complete.

If your focus is on getting through the Divorce with the least amount of financial consequence and emotional damage, then everything you say must be said with the end in mind.

It's more of a mindset during your conversations, like this:

"I don't need to remind him how much less we have after paying his tax debt... That money no longer exists; let's move on."

"Yes, I want equal parenting time. If the kids want to be with her every Sunday night during the school year, I highly doubt that will impact my relationship with the kids. Let's do what is easiest for everyone."

"When this is over, I'm not going to want any of "our" stuff. I'll get new towels, chairs - bed! I'm not fighting over that stuff."

See the end of the Divorce as the beginning of your new life. Work to Get Out in the most time-efficient and cost-effective way possible, always asking yourself, when this is over how much will _______ mean to me?

Now that you know Divorce is your only solution and have a better grasp on what to think and how to speak to one another while going through your Divorce, you are ready to start gathering the information you need before making any agreements.

INFORMATION GATHERING & THE DISCLOSURE PROCESS

The most critical part of your divorce is thoroughly gathering information.

If you rush through this part, fail to document, or disclose everything of marital value, then you could end up with a drawn-out process or back-in-court later situation.

Gathering information is tedious, but it doesn't have to be difficult.

This method for gathering your financial information is the same method our trained professionals use when a client retains our Divorce attorneys to help them.

Get the latest credit report for each of you. The credit report is the easiest way to see what debts are in whose name and what information is needed to complete your financial statements accurately.

Just as important as the financial statement are the mandatory disclosures you must exchange. These are the documents that detail the financial picture of your marriage.

Mandatory Disclosures in Colorado include the following.

<u>Income Tax Returns</u> (Most Recent 3 Years). Including W-2's, 1099's and K 1's, copies of extension requests, and estimated tax payments.

<u>Personal Financial Statements</u> (Last 3 Years).

All personal financial statements, statements of assets or liabilities, and credit and loan applications prepared during the last three years.

<u>Business Financial Statements</u> (Last 3 Years).

The last three fiscal years' financial statements, all year-to-date financial statements, and the same periodic financial statements for the prior year for any business in which you have an interest.

<u>Real Estate Documents</u>

The title documents and all documents stating the value of all real property in which a party has a personal or business interest.

<u>Personal Debt.</u>

All documents that reflect debt, and the most recent debt statements showing the balance and payment terms.

<u>Investments.</u>

Most recent documents identifying each investment and stating the current value.

<u>Employment Benefits.</u>

Most recent documents identifying each employment benefit and stating the current value.

Retirement Plans.

Most recent documents identifying each retirement plan, and stating the current value, and all Plan Summary Descriptions.

Bank/Financial Institution Accounts.

Most recent documents identifying each account at banks and other financial institutions and stating the current value.

Income Documentation.

For each income source in the current and prior calendar year, including income from employment, investment, government programs, gifts, trust distributions, prizes, and income from every other source, provide pay stubs, a current income statement and the final income statement for the prior year. Each self-employed party shall provide a sworn statement of gross income, business expenses necessary to produce income, and net income for the three months before the filing of the petition or post-decree motion.

Employment and Education-Related Child Care Documentation.

Documents that show average monthly employment-related childcare expenses, including childcare expenses related to parents' education and job search.

Insurance Documentation.

Life, health, and property insurance policies and current documents that show beneficiaries, coverage, cost, including the portion payable to provide health insurance for children, and payment schedule.

<u>Extraordinary Children's Expense Documentation</u>. The Documents that show the average monthly expense for all recurring extraordinary children's expenses.

Some of these documents may not apply to you. You do not have to invent anything that does not exist.

Not everyone has children, so those without kids won't have children's expense documentation. Others may not have personal financial statements that they maintain separately from their business documents.

If you both have the same access to accounts and information and you are both ok with not printing a hard copy, you don't need to do it. You only need to verify that you did have access to everything and considered it before entering into your Separation Agreement.

Remember the Fiduciary Duty you have to one another. Also, know that the fact-gathering process is not when you start negotiating your Divorce. Just gather all the information first, so everyone has the facts and numbers when you do start negotiating.

It is also not the time to start moving money or closing existing accounts. Doing so could make matters more difficult and complicated if you both don't understand what is happening.

Take time now to gather the information before moving on to the next chapter about preparing your financial statements.

DRAFTING YOUR FINANCIAL STATEMENTS ACCURATELY

Now you have what you need to draft your Financial Statement. Your Financial Statements are usually an 8-10-page state form that the Court reviews to understand your current financial situation. This helps you and the Court determine that your Separation Agreement is fair and equitable.

By having these disclosures and documents available, filling out your financial statement becomes much more manageable.

In Colorado, the financial statement addresses the following:

- Income information
- Deductions from your income
- Monthly Expenses
- Debts
- Real Estate
- Motor Vehicles
- Bank Accounts & Cash on Hand
- Life Insurance
- Furniture, Household Goods & Personal Property
- Investments
- Retirement

- Miscellaneous Assets
- Separate Property Interests

While much of this form seems self-explanatory, here are some general insights and guidance for each section. We'll discuss more in-depth when we work on drafting the Agreements.

INCOME

If you are paid by the hour, then you should easily be able to calculate your hourly rate with regular hours worked. If you are a salaried employee, then you need to make sure you are calculating monthly gross income - not weekly income or income per pay period. Gross income is the amount you earn before taxes or deductions apply.

If you are self-employed with a base salary, but also take draws or earn commissions, the best rule of thumb is to calculate your monthly gross income received over the past six months and average it. Then add a note that explains how you calculated your income. Depending on how and when you get paid, you may have to average the past 12 months or year to date.

You must list all the sources of your income on your sworn financial statement. Disclosing all of your income does not mean every source is considered to calculate support, but full disclosure is critical.

DEDUCTIONS

If you receive a paycheck regularly, most of the deductions will appear on your paystub. Make sure you are calculating the *monthly* amount and not per pay period.

If you are self-employed and do not get paid regularly, then you have options.

Use the amounts withheld for your taxes last year;

Talk to a CPA who can tell you what these deductions should be depending upon how much you are paid on your earnings- that you will eventually have to pay;

Leave it blank or mark as TBD (To Be Determined) if you don't regularly withhold from your pay.

Your financial statement should include everything for the court to consider at a later date, if necessary.

MONTHLY EXPENSES

Monthly expenses are probably the most shocking and often eye-opening part of the financial statements for couples. Either they haven't paid attention to the monthly amounts spent, or they get so frustrated estimating new costs once they have separate expenses.

If you have already separated, then most of these can be listed as separate expenses. If you still live together but have a method of who pays what, then let your financial statements reflect what you are currently doing. If you pay everything together, you may choose to claim the entire expense or divide the payment proportionate to incomes.

You will sign this legal document and file it with the court. You will represent that you are providing valid and accurate information to the best of your knowledge. If there is an expense or value, you don't know write "unknown" or TBD (To Be Determined) instead of guessing the amount not supported with documentation.

DEBTS

The Debt section is where you will put your credit reports to use.

Be sure to include:

- ✓ The correct name of creditor,
- ✓ The last four digits of the account number,
- ✓ Whose name is on the account; and
- ✓ The monthly minimum and total owed.

Having this accurate information when you start the Divorce can be significant if the Divorce is drawn out for any reason. You may need to know the date of separation amounts to better determine debts or increase in values in the most fair and equitable way possible when you finalize the divorce. Although technically still marital, there are negotiations to have about increases that were not *"for the benefit of the marriage."*

It is also wise to get date-of-marriage statements and determine the pre-marital values and, thus, separate property.

ASSETS

Now that we've determined and disclosed expenses and monthly costs that you have, it is time to detail your assets.

For your home, unless you agree on a value, it is OK to write "unknown" for the estimated value until you decide on an amount or have the home appraised.

For motor vehicles, use Kelley Blue Book to determine the value of the car. You can decide whether it is most likely that you would trade the car in or sell it on your own to calculate how much it is worth.

Expect the amounts in the checking accounts to vary from the date you sign the financial statement to when it's filed, to when the court reviews the financial statement and other pleadings. The sooner the two of you can figure out how to pay for joint expenses through the process while separating bank accounts, the better.

Once you file the Petition for Dissolution of Marriage with the court, neither spouse can transfer money, change or close accounts without the written agreement of the other.

INVESTMENTS & RETIREMENT ACCOUNTS

If you have investment and retirement accounts, don't assume that the current value on your monthly or quarterly statement is the actual marital value of the account. There can be complex equations to determine how much of the account value, that you cannot collect until you retire is marital and what will be your separate property based upon the date of divorce.

Especially with Public Employment Retirement Accounts (PERA) and military pensions, consider having a professional determine the marital value of the account. To know the marital value is, is to have options for asset allocation during settlement.

MISCELLANEOUS ASSETS

Many also do not try and figure out the values of personal property and household goods unless there are high price items such as artwork or antiques. Unless agreed otherwise, the engagement ring and wedding bands are considered gifts to the other. Often there are other jewelry, tools, art, heirlooms that are of substantial value that you should appraise to determine how much the items are worth.

Otherwise, it is common to value everything as if you were going to sell it on-line this weekend. Be reasonable.

Be aware that you may be held to the value you place on your assets. Be reasonable and stay conservative.

The need to have your financial statements complete with all information is essential for drafting comprehensive agreements.

If you drafted your Sworn Financial Statement and find there is a lot of numbers unknown or to be determined, take the time now to get these answers.

After taking the time to thoroughly gather, exchange, and share your financial information, you are ready to draft and negotiate comprehensive and reliable Separation Agreements and Parenting Plans.

DETERMINING THE BEST DIVISION OF YOUR DEBTS & ASSETS

Assets and debts may not be divided equally, but fair and equitably.

While this DIY Guide may spare you from as much legal and technical language as possible, knowing what the law says is helpful and necessary before dividing your assets and debts.

Colorado Revised Statute § 14-10-113 determines the Division of Marital Property as follows.

... the court shall divide the marital property, without regard to marital misconduct, in such proportions as the court deems just after considering all relevant factors including:

The contribution of each spouse to the acquisition of the marital property, including the contribution of a spouse as homemaker;

The value of the property set apart to each spouse;

The economic circumstances of each spouse at the time the division of property is to become effective, including the desirability of awarding the family home or the right to live therein for reasonable periods to the spouse with whom any children reside the majority of the time;

and

Any increases or decreases in the value of the separate property of the spouse during the marriage or the depletion of the separate property for marital purposes.

(2) For purposes of this article only, and subject to the provisions of subsection (7) of this section, "marital property" means all property acquired by either spouse after the marriage except:

Property acquired by gift, bequest, devise, or descent;

Property acquired in exchange for property acquired before the marriage or in exchange for property acquired by gift, bequest, devise, or descent;

Property acquired by a spouse after a decree of legal separation; and

Property excluded by valid agreement of the parties.

Now that you better understand – or at least read - how Colorado law defines marital property, let's design your Asset-Debt Worksheet. (ADW) The ADW is a spreadsheet that calculates the division of your assets and debts. By taking the time to create your worksheet, you will have the perfect tool to evaluate different ideas for dividing the assets and debts.

Here is what the Asset Debt Worksheet looks like:

Assets	Title	Value	Debt	Net	NAME Separate	NAME Separate	NAME Marital	NAME Marital
Real Property								
Subtotal								
Vehicle(s)								
Subtotal			$0.00	$0.00	$0.00	$0.00	$0.00	$0.00
Bank Account(s)								
Subtotal		$0.00		$0.00	$0.00	$0.00	$0.00	$0.00
Retirement/Pension(s):								
Subtotal								
Stocks/Bonds/Investments								
Subtotal		$0.00		$0.00	$0.00	$0.00	$0.00	$0.00
Business Interests:								
Subtotal				$0.00	$0.00	$0.00	$0.00	$0.00
Other Asset(s)								
Subtotal		$0.00		$0.00	$0.00	$0.00	$0.00	$0.00
Total Assets								
Percentages								
Debts			OWED					
Total Debt			$0.00		$0.00	$0.00	$0.00	$0.00
Percentages								
TOTAL ASSET/DEBT								

Each item has a row. If you have one home, then there is one line for the property and one line for the total value of the asset. If you have three houses, you will have four rows.

For Motor Vehicles, there may be two cars, a trailer, a boat? These are each listed in separate rows.

At the bottom of each section, you will have a TOTAL ROW. This chart above demonstrates the total rows.

REAL ESTATE

Real estate is your home or any real property one, or both of you currently own. If you rent your home and do not have other real property, this section may not apply and remain blank.

Say you have real estate with a current agreed-upon value of $500,000.00. The mortgage or amount still owed against the property is $200,000.00. You have roughly $300,000.00 of marital equity to divide. If you will sell the house and plan to share the proceeds equally, add half of the total equity or $150,000.00 to each spouse's column.

In other cases, one spouse may keep the home and the equity and trade different assets for the other's portion of marital equity in the house.

If either spouse owned a home or the marital home *before the marriage*, that spouse might have a pre-marital property interest not included as marital property. List the value under separate property instead. If the value of the property increased during the marriage, the increase in value is considered marital and should be shared or credited accordingly.

It's important to note that some couples figure out what the net proceeds will be before entering the amount into the worksheet. They take out the cost of sale, the broker percentages, possibly the costs of repair before the sale, and then calculate the amount that they can reasonably expect to receive after the sale. Others figure since the amount will be divided equally and is not known when drafting the ADW, gross amounts are fine to use to determine the reasonable property division.

MOTOR VEHICLES

This section will include the cars you have, any motorbikes, boats, four-wheelers, snowmobiles, etc.

Once you determine car values either by agreement or with Kelley Blue Book and have current loan statements, you will enter the information for each.

Couples usually decide to keep the car they drove during the marriage.

Sometimes couples decide to pay off the car debt from the equity they receive from the home. Others trade-in or sell the cars before dividing the assets and debt.

Whatever car you decide to keep, make sure of the following before deciding to keep it.

Is the car in good condition, or will it need significant work soon?

How much are gasoline and maintenance going to be each month?

What are the insurance and tax/registration fees each year?

Once you Divorce, these will be separate expenses, so make sure you understand when you want the car that you can afford everything that comes with it.

For each car, fill in the worksheet by listing current value, amount of debt still to be paid on any car loans, and then the net marital equity value in the column of the spouse keeping the respective motor vehicle.

Keep in mind, not every section has to be equal.

BANK ACCOUNTS

It is common and understood that bank accounts fluctuate regularly with expenses and paydays. Make sure everyone knows exactly where the money is going, and what you plan to pay separately if you decide to keep joint accounts during the Divorce. So long as you divide the accounts before filing for Divorce or agree in writing to separate them during the Divorce, you can do that.

- Do not move money or close accounts;
- Do not change insurance;
- Do not modify or cash in retirement;
- Do not sell anything that is marital;

Once you file the Petition for Dissolution of Marriage, you must have a written agreement to move or change anything you are doing financially during the Divorce. Unless you have written agreements to do any of the above while the Divorce is pending, you must wait until everything is final.

If you divided the accounts already, enter the information as a marital account allocated to the spouse who now has the account or monies in it. If you plan to share the amounts equally and then close the account, then enter half the value to each person on the asset-debt worksheet.

INVESTMENTS

Investments can be very complex or very simple.

Whatever the value of the account was at the date of marriage is the separate property of that spouse. As an example, you may have a separate property interest of $25,000.00. The interest could be something you had before the marriage, or inheritance, or a gift just to you. This amount would be listed under assets and then placed in your separate property column instead of in your marital property column.

Expect to divide the retirement accounts equally even if one spouse contributes more to retirement during the marriage, while you share the other spouse's income for daily living expenses.

The division of investments can be difficult if there is an employer, business, or a partnership interest involved. There are often pensions and retirement structures that won't payout until one spouse retires that could be many years after the divorce is final.

Some couples have to cash in investments to pay the other spouse their share of the asset value. Cashing in any investments could have penalty and tax consequences that significantly change the amount you lose for the transaction.

If there are business interests, and levels of contribution are not similar, do not expect to divide the value equally automatically. Do what is fair and equitable.

Whether business interests, retirement accounts, pensions, PERAs, or other investments, take the time to consult with a CPA or financial advisor to understand what you have. They can also advise you about the best way to divide the assets.

Some investments are too good to be divided. Just because you are divorcing doesn't mean you necessarily have to lose your joint interest. With property, some couples keep the house and title it to the kids. With businesses, some couples divorce and then meet with a business attorney to design better partnership and operating agreements. Still, others structure 5 to 10-year buyout plans so the investment can continue to grow even after the marriage is over.

If you decide to maintain the asset jointly, then either place each party's percentage of estimated value in each marital value column or leave it off the spreadsheet since you won't be dividing it.

MISCELLANEOUS ASSETS

Miscellaneous assets are the catch-all. Everything from frequent flyer miles, to coins or family trusts, that may or may not have a marital interest may be considered a miscellaneous asset. If there is an asset with value and it does not fit in any of the categories, list it here.

Keep in mind that some couples have savings accounts for the kids or buy their kid a car. Often, we disclose the accounts and note that they are and will remain in the children's property and are not considered marital assets. Other items in the miscellaneous column include mileage and hotel points or rewards or timeshares that do not necessarily have a value per se.

DEBTS

Because you accounted for the mortgage and car loans above, do not include the amounts owed a second time on the Asset Debt Worksheet.

Under debts should be everything you each listed as debts in your financial statements.

Be careful to consider what debt incurred for the benefit of the marriage or personal interest. If there are student loans, business debts, or loans from family members, these may be separate debt, but for now, include all the amounts outstanding and who you think should have the obligation after the divorce.

The assumption is anything that accrued during the marriage is marital debt. If you can negotiate and agree that one person is responsible for the liability and it was not for the benefit of the marriage, then it may be listed as a separate debt, instead of marital debt.

When deciding who is taking what debt, make sure you understand the minimum payments due, and the interest rates involved. Make sure you've discussed the possible effects on your credit when deciding to close a joint account. Try to find a way to use other assets to pay off the debt so you can both leave the marriage as clean as possible.

Starting over is already hard enough.

EQUALIZATION

Colorado law requires the fair and equitable allocation of marital debts and assets.

By entering all your assets and debts from your sworn financial statements into the asset-debt worksheet, and then separating values into each spouse's column as you choose to divide them, you will be able to see how much of the marital property and debt each spouse may receive.

By dividing the amount, each spouse will take by the total value, you will see how close the division is to 50/50.

By way of example. Imagine you have $800,000.00 of total *net* asset value after subtracting the amounts of any debt remaining. Through the allocation of real estate, motor vehicles, accounts, and investments, and any other assets, say you have $380,000, and your spouse keeps the other $420,000.

$380,000/$800,000 = 47.5%

$420,000/$800,000 = 52.5%

$20,000 would equalize the division of assets and debts in this instance. Your spouse would pay you $20,000 from somewhere for you each to have an equal amount of the assets and debt division.

There may or may not be reasons for an unequal division of assets.

This calculation also does not factor in separate property interests such as pre-marital values or inheritance you may have received during the divorce.

Once you decide how to divide the assets and know who will be responsible for what debt, it is time to consider spousal support.

SPOUSAL SUPPORT

In Colorado, spousal support or alimony is known as "maintenance." If there has been a significant difference between the incomes of each spouse during the marriage, then Colorado law will consider if the higher wage-earner has a duty to continue to support the spouse earning less or not working during the marriage.

Colorado established new presumptive guidelines in 2014 for courts and litigants to have a framework to determine fair and equitable maintenance awards. In 2019, the law changed again, now making maintenance, like child support, so the payor does not receive credit or a deduction for the amount paid, and the spouse receiving maintenance does not have to claim the payment as income.

Colorado Revised Statute §14-10-114 provides detail regarding maintenance. For a determination of maintenance, the Court considers the following:

- The amount of each party's gross income;
- The marital property apportioned to each party;
- The financial resources of each party – actual and potential,
- Reasonable financial need as established during the marriage.

The statutory language and the award of maintenance, however, is *still* left to the discretion of the Court if you can't determine what is fair and equitable.

There are three different phases of calculating maintenance in Colorado.

Per *Colorado Revised Statutes §14-10-114*: If the duration of the marriage is at least three years and the parties' combined annual adjusted gross income does not exceed $240,000, this is how to calculate maintenance.

If maintenance is **deductible for federal income tax purposes by the payor and taxable to the party receiving maintenance**, then the guidelines advise calculating maintenance by taking 40% of the parties' combined monthly adjusted gross income minus the lower-income party's monthly adjusted gross income.

If the maintenance is **not** tax-deductible to payor and **not** taxable to spouse receiving support, and the parties' combined monthly adjusted gross is $10,000 or less, then presumptive maintenance is 80% of the amount calculated above.

If the maintenance is **not** tax-deductible to the payor and **not** taxable to the party receiving maintenance, and the parties combined monthly gross income is between $10,000 and $20,000 then use 75% of the amount calculated in #1 above.

If your combined income is more than $20,000 per month or $240,000 per year, then the guideline amount may not apply. You will have to consider the needs of the spouse earning less and the lifestyle you shared during your marriage.

Hopefully seeing this in numbers will make more sense:

#1. MAINTENANCE IS TAX-DEDUCTIBLE, AND COMBINED MONTHLY GROSS INCOME IS MORE THAN $10,000.00:

You earn $10,000.00/month. Spouse earns $3500.00 per month.
Your combined monthly gross income is $13,500.00 per month.
40% of your combined monthly gross income is $13,500 x .4 = $5400.00
$5400.00 - $3500.00 = Monthly Maintenance of $1900.00/month.
Per the presumptive guideline maintenance, you will pay your spouse is $1900.00 per month.

#2 MAINTENANCE IS NOT TAX DEDUCTIBLE, NOR TAXABLE, AND COMBINED MONTHLY GROSS INCOME IS LESS THAN $10,000.

You now earn $7500.00/month Spouse earns $2000.00 per month.
Your combined monthly gross income is $9500.00 per month.
40% of your combined monthly gross income is $9500 x .4 = $3800.00
$3800.00 - $2000.00 = $1800.00
80% of $1800 = $1440.00
The presumptive guideline maintenance you will pay your spouse is $1440.00 per month.

#3 MAINTENANCE IS NOT TAX DEDUCTIBLE, NOT TAXABLE AND COMBINED MONTHLY GROSS INCOME IS BETWEEN $10,000 AND $20,000 PER MONTH.

Same facts as #1 above:
You earn $10,000.00/month Spouse earns $3500.00 per month.
Your combined monthly gross income is $13,500.00 per month.
40% of your combined monthly gross income is $13,500 x .4 = $5400.00
$5400.00 - $3500.00 = $1900.00
75% of $1900.00 = $1425.00
The presumptive guideline for maintenance to be paid by you to your spouse is $1425.00 per month.

The second part of the presumptive maintenance equation is how long should you pay or receive maintenance. If you've been married less than three years, do not expect to pay or receive maintenance. After three years of marriage, *Colorado Revised Statute §14-10-114* provides a chart by months of marriage to determine how long to pay maintenance. The length of time can be anywhere from 30% to 50% of the months married.

According to the chart within *Colorado Revised Statute §14-10-114*, if you've been married seven years or 84 months, the guidelines suggest you pay or receive maintenance for the next 33 months – or 39% of the length of the marriage.

If you've been married 15 years or 180 months, then the guidelines suggest you pay or receive maintenance for the next 90 months. Any marriage over 12 and a half years results in the presumption that maintenance is paid for a period equal to half the life of the marriage.

Also, know that if one spouse is not earning as much as they are capable of making, then the amount that they *are capable* of earning for a 40-hour workweek may be used to calculate maintenance. In other words, if you've had a job making a monthly gross income of $10,000 until recently, and you are now earning $6000.00 a month, a possible award of maintenance may be calculated using $10,000 for your income.

The formula for maintenance is only a *guideline* and not absolute.

Many couples have incomes that exceed the guidelines for support, meaning their combined gross income exceeds $20,000, or there are certain financial factors for the parties to consider. The point to remember is that the payment of support, just like the division of assets, should be fair and equitable.

You may be in a situation that you can settle the property or debt division that saves you from paying or receiving maintenance. If the one getting paid remarries, spousal support ends.

If you are the one paying support, try and negotiate that if your soon to be former spouse decides to live with a significant other that is financially contributing to his new life, then you will not be obligated to support him any longer.

If you contract for it, then that too will terminate the payment of maintenance. Too often, the spouse receiving maintenance will move in with another and start a great life, all while collecting a maintenance check because technically they are not married.

Some couples decide to pay the maintenance through the property settlement. Here is an example: The couple determines that the maintenance would be $2500 for four years, or $120,000.00. Payor Spouse gives Spouse to receive maintenance $120,000.00 more of the equity in the home and then doesn't pay maintenance.

Maybe you negotiate payment of more of the marital debt in exchange for paying or receiving maintenance.

Maintenance may be a difficult part of your separation. Be reasonable, empathetic, and forward-thinking. Consider how you lived while married as well as the fact that there are now two separate households to support with similar income that supported one home during the marriage.

The goal of divorce is to be done, not to have to continue to support or to rely on your Ex for support financially.

Now that you have...

- Decided Divorce is the best option
- Gathered all your financial information
- Completed your financial statement and certificate of compliance
- Drafted your Asset - Debt spreadsheet
- Considered how to divide the assets and debts
- Determined if and how much spousal support will be

YOU ARE READY TO DRAFT THE SEPARATION AGREEMENT!

It's time to add the words to the numbers. Getting through the numbers and seeing how much everything is worth and how much debt there may be is so difficult.

Drafting the language to match precisely the agreement you are making is very important. Do not rush through this part. Again, working with an attorney to help you draft legally sound documents is always advised.

If you still choose to Do It Yourself, the language and explanations following will be helpful.

Let's draft your Separation Agreement!

DRAFTING CLEAR & CONCISE AGREEMENTS

As you can see from the information and options discussed, there is so much to think about before drafting agreements. Remember, you are about to prepare a legally binding contract. A consultation with an attorney before, during, or after you draft your agreements is a very good idea.

If you are still planning to draft the Separation Agreement on your own, use your financial statement as the outline to detail the information and topics in your Separation Agreement.

A sample Separation Agreement is at the end of this Guide. Review it now to better understand and follow along.

In this chapter, we will walk through each step and paragraph of the Separation Agreement, so you will better understand what to include as well as why it's necessary.

The language of the Draft Agreement is in bold-face type. The explanation is in a different font, so it's easier to follow.

Remember, this is a Guide to help you understand what you are doing if you choose to move forward without attorneys. This information is not legal advice or in any way offering you more than a better understanding of what is in your Agreements and why.

THE CAPTION

<table>
<tr><td>DISTRICT COURT, __________ COUNTY,
STATE OF COLORADO
ADDRESS
PHONE NUMBER
____

In re the Marriage of:

Petitioner: JANE SMITH

and

Respondent: JOHN SMITH</td><td>▲COURT USE ONLY▲</td></tr>
<tr><td>JANE SMITH
Address
Phone
Email

JOHN SMITH
Address
Phone
Email</td><td>Case Number:

Division</td></tr>
<tr><td colspan="2">DOCUMENT NAME HERE</td></tr>
</table>

Almost every document filed with the court starts with the same case caption. The Caption includes the Court name and address and phone number; The name of the parties and their title – Petitioner, Co-Petitioner, or Respondent; the address of the parties or the party filing the document; the Case Number and Division, and the name of your pleading.

RECITALS

You will notice that each section of the Agreement should have a title for ease of reading and understanding.

Before you get to the main language of the Agreement, there are some necessary details to address first.

The introduction paragraphs, or "recitals," inform the reader about the marriage. There is certain information the Court needs to enter the divorce decree, and we often include the information in the recitals.

Start the Separation Agreement by introducing the parties to the Court.

(NAME), Petitioner, and (NAME), Co-Petitioner/Respondent, submit the following Separation Agreement regarding the settlement of their respective rights as to their property, debts, and spousal maintenance.

This paragraph introduces the name of the Parties as they appear on your Petition and explain what the contract will address.

If you file the Petition together, you will refer to yourselves as "Petitioner" and "Co-Petitioner." If instead one spouse files the Petition without the other, then refer to yourselves as "Petitioner" (the spouse who initially files the Petition) and "Respondent" (the spouse who receives the Petition or didn't file the original Petition.)

Recitals are introductory statements to your Agreement that are often included in your Decree when your divorce is final.

The Petition for Dissolution of Marriage was filed on (DATE) in the (NAME County), State of Colorado.

The dates are necessary to tell the Court that at least 91 days have passed when they enter the Decree and confirm jurisdiction is proper for the Court.

The Parties were married on (DATE) in (City & State). The parties separated on (DATE).

The length of the marriage may become important later in the Agreement. Documenting when and where the marriage occurred may be necessary for possible jurisdiction issues and potential support matters.

The parties are the biological parents of (number of minor children) minor children of the marriage.

(NAME), (DATE OF BIRTH)
(NAME), (DATE OF BIRTH)

Keep the Separation Agreement and Parenting Plan as separate documents. However, include the number of children involved and the name and birth date of each child in both documents. In Colorado, any child under the age of 19 is considered a minor child.

(Wife's NAME) is not pregnant.

The determination of pregnancy is a specific finding the Court makes when entering the decree. If one spouse is pregnant, then say it here. The Court will still enter the order, but you will be back for further allocation of parental responsibilities after the child is born.

Parties currently reside in NAME County, Colorado, and have lived in Colorado for at least 91 days before the filing of the Petition. They consent to this Court's jurisdiction over them personally and over the subject NAME County.

Information about how long the parties live in Colorado is also for the Divorce Decree. You must live in Colorado for at least three months before filing for divorce in Colorado for the Colorado Court to have jurisdiction. There have to be at least 91 days between when you file the Petition for Dissolution and the date the Court can enter the decree.

Parties recognize that their marriage is irretrievably broken.

In Colorado, the Court must determine that the marriage is truly over. Only one spouse must believe and declare that the marriage is over for the court to make this finding.

To avoid further litigation, the parties have agreed to the following decisions relating to the determination of maintenance, the division of marital assets, payment of marital debts, and attorney's fees. The parties request the agreements set forth herein become a Permanent

Order of the Court and that the Decree enter dissolving the marriage to one another.

This language tells the Court you have settled all issues to finalize the divorce.

Accordingly, the parties mutually agree as follows:

This language is to transition to the actual agreements.

By now, you introduced the parties, documented dates, and places and indicated you are offering this contract as a full and final settlement. Now we can draft the specific language of your Agreement.

Remember, by following your financial statement, you can make sure you cover everything in the most precise and concise way possible.

PROPERTY DIVISION

Property Division includes:

- The Real Estate you own;
- The Motor Vehicles;
- Cash and Bank Accounts;
- Investment & Retirement Accounts;
- Personal Property, Household Goods & Furnishings; and
- Business Interests.

While we addressed these when drafting the financial statement and Asset Debt Worksheet, we are now discussing the language used in your separation agreement.

Real Estate

For each property include the following:

- The property address;
- How the property is titled;
- What the agreed-upon value of the property is;
- Whether one spouse is keeping the home, or you will sell it;
- If selling the house, how to divide the costs of sale and net proceeds;
- How the mortgage, insurance, and expenses for the home will be paid until the home is sold;
- How to allocate the tax credits;
- If one spouse is keeping the home, how long they will have to refinance the house to remove the other spouse from the mortgage;
- What happens if they are not able to refinance the home in the time agreed upon;

For many families, the marital home is both the main asset and financial liability. Many think one party staying is best for the kids to keep some stability without really determining the financial consequence of maintaining the home after the divorce as a single parent.

Making sure to know the details of what you are doing with the home is so essential when drafting your agreements. Take the time to look at the monthly expense as much as the equity you may receive as well as the costs of closing or selling the home. Timing can be everything.

Here is the sample language.

MARITAL HOME LOCATED AT (ADDRESS)

The parties jointly own

OR

The home is titled in (Spouse's Name) name and (Name of one or both spouses) is named on the mortgage.

The current net value of the home is approximately $(home value)

(Name) shall keep the marital home as her/his sole and separate property. The equity in the home shall be allocated to (Name).

OR

The parties shall sell the Marital home.

The home shall be listed by (Date)

All costs to repair, list, and sell the home shall be divided equally/shared by (Name) paying X% and (Name) paying X%.

The mortgage, insurance, and other costs necessary shall be paid by (Name) OR shared equally.

The parties shall maintain joint account XXXX and contribute $_________ each not later than the 1st of each month for payment of their share.

If the home does not sell by (Date), parties shall agree to reduce the listing price as determined by the agent selling the home. Parties shall cooperate with signing all documents necessary for the sale of the home.

The net proceeds for the sale shall be divided as follows (Name) shall receive X%. (Name) shall receive X%.

(NAME) shall be responsible for all mortgage payments and living expenses from the date of decree forward.

(NAME) shall have (NUMBER) months to refinance the home into her name or otherwise sell the property.

The parties shall be solely and separately responsible for all living costs for their respective homes from DATE forward.

Both parties shall claim one-half of the tax credit for payment of

the mortgage interest for (year).

OR

(NAME) shall claim the mortgage interest for (Year).

For each property, walk through these same provisions and describe what will happen to the property and when. Be sure to be as detailed as possible, including deadlines, percentages of ownership, and division of proceeds, or how much one spouse is receiving if the equity is staying with the property.

Before drafting the language, make sure the person keeping the property can qualify to refinance it into his or her name.

If selling the property, you should also consult with a real estate agent to know what you should do for an optimal sale of the property and what a reasonable amount to expect from the sale.

Property taxes can be complicated, whether re-financing the home. Consulting with a Certified Public Accountant (CPA) can provide the language necessary to protect you from tax liability or better understand these costs associated with keeping or selling the home.

MOTOR VEHICLES

Be sure that you know the trade-in value, and the costs you will have in insurance and maintenance for the vehicles you want to keep. Know what the fees for registration each year will likely be and discuss the estimated costs of fuel and logistics for family transportation if that may be an issue after the divorce.

When discussing your cars, boats, four-wheelers, trailers, and snowmobiles, be able to look at the asset-debt worksheet you already designed and add the language you need:

- The make and model of the Vehicle;
- How it is titled or who holds the lease or loan; The agreed-upon value;
- Who is keeping the vehicle;
- If you are selling it, who is responsible for selling it and what happens to the proceeds;
- Who is responsible for future payments, insurance, maintenance, and taxes;

- Whether or not the other spouse is relieved of all future liability.

Here is an example:

(Name) shall keep the (MAKE & MODEL) as his/her sole and separate property. Parties agree that there is approximately $ __________________ of marital equity in the car. The equity shall be allocated to (Name).

(NAME) shall have (Number) months to refinance the car loan into his/her name.

(NAME) hereby assumes all financial responsibility for his car, including but not limited to auto insurance and car maintenance.

(NAME) hereby indemnifies (Name) of any and all financial responsibility or any other liability for the (MAKE & MODEL).

If you agree to sell the vehicle, here is the proposed language:

The parties shall sell the (YEAR, MAKE & MODEL) (NAME) shall choose the dealership and negotiate the price of sale. All proceeds shall be used toward the marital debt

OR

(NAME) shall receive X% of the proceeds from the sale and (NAME) shall receive X% of the proceeds from the sale.

In many cases, one spouse may take responsibility for the car through the divorce. They then may sell it or trade it in on their terms later, knowing that they will keep the proceeds or benefit from a trade-in.

Someone keeping the car is a much easier process than trying to stipulate to a sale and share of any proceeds later.

If you lease your vehicles, then there is not marital value. When the car is under a lease, detail the language about when the lease expires if the contract needs to be re-negotiated into another's name within a certain amount of time, detail those agreements too. Make sure the person responsible for all payments is listed and that the other spouse is relieved from any further responsibility, or "indemnified."

Now that you know what happens with the vehicles, you are ready to detail your agreements about the cash & bank accounts.

CASH & BANK ACCOUNTS

Amounts in the bank accounts and investment accounts can change during the Divorce. Be sure to give a date certain for the values you are contemplating. If anything changes drastically before the divorce is final, you need to be able to see what account has changed, and where funds may have gone.

Meet with your banker to understand the language necessary to remove names from accounts and best understand how to transfer balances, or possibly share a joint account for children's expenses.

Dividing accounts during or after divorce is a great time to go over bank fees and service charges, understand account minimums and limits. Often spouses keep accounts at the same bank where they had marital accounts.

Others take this opportunity to find a new bank and don't like the idea of having accounts that could be mistaken for their spouse's account after divorce.

When you draft the language for your Separation Agreement include the following information.

For each Bank Account write down the Name of Bank, what kind of account it is, and last four digits of every bank account;

(BANK NAME) Checking Account (XX1234)

Whose name is on the account - both spouses or just one?

(XX1234) is held jointly by both parties

OR

XX1234 is titled in (NAME's) name

How much is in the account as of a specific date?

As of (DATE) there is $ _____________ in the account.

Will you keep the account in both names, close it, or transfer to one person or the other?

If you keep the account together, how will fees be shared, who can take what, who adds how much, and when?

For purposes of (reason child support/property maintenance/etc.) The parties will continue to hold the account jointly.

Each month (NAME) shall deposit $_______________ into the account by (DATE) as and for (REASON). Costs associated with

maintaining the account shall be shared equally OR ***paid by (NAME).***

*Only consider sharing a bank account after divorce when sharing children's expenses or continuing to manage a business or property together after the divorce.

How will the account be divided, and by when?

How soon after you sign your agreement must the account be closed or transferred?

(NAME) will keep the account as his sole and separate property. All amounts remaining in the account shall be allocated to (NAME).

OR

Account XX1234 shall be closed within 30 days of signing this Agreement. Any amounts remaining in the account shall be shared with (NAME) receiving $ ______________ and (NAME) receiving $______________.

Finally, we have the language about the deadline for closing or transferring the account. Thirty to Sixty days is a typical deadline, so everyone can make sure that autopay and EFTs are correctly set up.

The best practice is to walk through each of these steps for every account you have and divide or allocate to one spouse or the other.

Some families have investment and retirement accounts to divide. Handle these separate from bank accounts as they usually have significantly more to divide and may need special orders from the court to allocate correctly.

Now we can discuss investment and retirement accounts.

INVESTMENT & RETIREMENT ACCOUNTS

If you have significant accounts to divide, or don't know anything about your investments, meet with a financial advisor to discuss how transfers from the accounts should happen. If any of the investment accounts need Qualified Domestic Relations Orders (QDRO), this may cost more and require a separate professional to draft.

The Financial Advisor can also tell you if there are definite benefits to keeping, sharing, or changing the investment structures after the divorce, and how to best determine the current value.

Accounts like Public Employee Retirement Accounts (PERAs), pensions, or other retirement accounts may not be divided after the Divorce. Each spouse may receive an amount when the spouse retires instead of immediately after the divorce.

Because of this, it is so important to understand that the amount reflected as the current value on your monthly or quarterly statement is different from the marital value at the time of retirement. I've known clients to lose hundreds of thousands of dollars for not having the account properly valued at the time of divorce. Once you sign the Agreement, you don't get to try and recover the amounts you should have taken during the divorce later.

When dividing retirement, try and keep as many of the accounts intact as possible. Try to allocate entire accounts to one spouse or the other and then determine an amount from a single account to be transferred to make things equal if necessary.

The objective is to keep the divorce as clean and as simple as possible. If you try and start transferring one half the amount from several different accounts, the language of the agreement and keeping track of everything can get complicated.

When drafting the language and detail, you need to include the following:

- Name of the account and last four digits of the account number?
- How is the account titled?
- What is the marital value of the account?
- Who will keep the account, or how will it be divided?

Here are some Examples:

(NAME) currently has (NAME & ACCOUNT TYPE) The value of the accounts collectively is currently$ ________________.

He/She also has a (NAME & ACCOUNT TYPE) with a marital value of $ _________. He/She shall maintain the accounts as her separate property. The amounts accrued for purposes of her retirement shall remain her sole and separate property.

(NAME) currently has a retirement account #*(last 4 digits)*

with *(NAME OF INVESTMENT COMPANY).* The account value was $______________ as of *(DATE).*

He also has a *(NAME OF COMPANY)* account # *(last 4 digits)* with a balance of $ ___________. He shall keep the accounts and the amounts in each account as his sole and separate property.

The parties have a ______________(kind of account) known as (Name and Account Number.) (Account name and Number) shall be divided equally.

All costs necessary for the preparation of a Qualified Domestic Relations Order shall be shared equally.

The transfer shall occur no later than X months after the entry of the decree.

Any increase in value or decrease from the date of the decree to transfer shall be shared equally between the parties.

After the investment and retirement accounts are shared and divided, you should next address any business interests.

In addition to investments and retirement accounts, there may be business interests to divide.

BUSINESS INTERESTS

In today's world of entrepreneurship, network marketing, and side hustle businesses, many couples have business interests to divide. These business interests can scale from millions of dollars to no value at all.

If there is a business that was established during the marriage or continued during the marriage, and no one is sure of the value, there are expert business appraisers and evaluators to help. When determining the value of a company, first discuss and understand whether or not someone is keeping the business, or the business will be sold in light of the divorce.

If one spouse keeps the business, then you need to determine the investment value of the business. The investment value may be different than a realistic sale price for the same company.

Some couples decide to determine the business value with the help of a Certified Public Accountant (CPA). A CPA can review tax returns, balance sheets, and profit and loss statements to determine agreeable business value.

Others decide that the business is a service business, and there is not a value separate from the income the spouse-owner is earning.

Once you agree upon value for any business interests, you will include the following in your Separation Agreement

- Name of business and date the company started;
- What the determined value of the business is;
- How to divide the business interests; and
- Any details of payment to the receiving spouse.

Here are some examples:

NAME OF BUSINESS was established on or about (Date) Parties agree that the business entity has a marital value of $________________. For purposes of allocation of marital Property.

(Name) shall keep the business as his sole and separate property. $____________ (Name) shall be credited to (Name) for purposes of allocation of the marital property.

OR

The parties agree not to value the business, nor do they believe there is a marital value for purposes of division of the marital estate.

(Name) shall maintain the business as his sole and separate property.

(Name) waives any further claim to a marital interest in the business.

In consideration for the payments described, (Name) waives all interests in (name) businesses with her signature below.

(Name) hereby indemnifies and holds (Name) harmless of any financial responsibility and all liability that may result from actions preceding the dissolution of marriage, or in the future as they may pertain to his businesses.

This is very general language, only describing 2 of many possibilities when considering business valuations.

There may be business operating agreements or partnership documents that limit a spouse's right to any ownership interest in the business.

There may be payment structures that save a disproportionate allocation of the marital estate.

Be careful and consult the proper professionals before agreeing to anything or signing anything when dividing business interests during your Divorce.

What is left, you ask? The "things!" Personal property. Personal property is everything from clothes and jewelry to tools and furniture. Sometimes this is no big deal for couples to divide, and other times it can be everything.

PERSONAL PROPERTY

Now that we know who is keeping the family business, who gets the couch? The last part of the property settlement is the language that details who gets the "stuff."

Remember, inheritance, whether financial or items, is not considered a marital asset.

The engagement and wedding rings are considered gifts to the spouse who received the rings unless you determined otherwise in writing.

Be realistic when valuing personal property. The rule of thumb for setting a value when you don't know is to decide how much could you sell it for this weekend on Craigslist or during your "*Getting Divorced Yard Sale.*"

Most couples can divide household goods without much detail or concern. Others have furniture, art, jewelry, tools, equipment, or animals such as horses that have significant value. The financial statements should include items of importance or considerable value.

If the Agreement is silent to an item, it will likely stay with the spouse who has it when your divorce is final. If you separated sometime before drafting the agreement, hopefully, you divided the personal property then. If not, agree to a time to walk through the home together and determine if there are items you may have forgotten about or think should be valued.

Here are some examples of the language regarding personal property and household goods.

While (Name) moved from the home with a substantial amount of the furniture. He is only in temporary living space that has not permitted the taking of some items.

(Name) shall remove his personal belongings remaining household goods and furnishings no later than ___________ (Date).

Any disputed items shall remain in the home until the parties can arbitrate the values and disposition of remaining items.

OR

The parties will divide all personal property among themselves outside of this Agreement.

If the parties are unable to agree on property division, they shall participate in arbitration or mediation to resolve any disputes.

OR

(Name) shall receive credit in the amount of $___________ for her share of all household furnishings, goods, and tools that remain in the marital home. (Name) waives any further interest in the personal property or household goods.

Some couples attach lists of the property they agree each will have to the Separation Agreement.

WHO GETS THE DOG?

Under the division of personal property, we often include what happens to the family pets. Many times, couples arrange animal parenting time and continue to share the animals. Others forfeit the animal, and one spouse will keep the pets. Still, other couples agree that the animal is really for the benefit of the children, and the pet goes with them between homes.

Whatever you decide to do with your pets, it is good to state the agreement in your contract.

Now that you described everything you own, detailed and divided the assets and property, you can draft the language regarding the marital debt.

There are usually monthly minimum payments to consider when detailing your expenses.

We discuss the debts after the property allocation in the separation agreement because the property division is often more complex and detailed than the division of marital debt.

MARITAL DEBTS

Before deciding who is taking what debts, think about what you can pay off with marital assets. Considerations when dividing debt include, the interest rates for each card if there are rewards points to share, and who uses the card most often.

There may be a concern that if you canceled cards or accounts you have had for a long time, your credit might be affected.

Discuss this with the card company or with a financial advisor before deciding what debts to take.

Some companies will issue new cards and account numbers to each spouse separately. Other companies will make you close the accounts and start new accounts if you choose. Every company can be very different, so make sure to talk to your lenders and creditors before deciding how you are going to divide the marital debt.

If one spouse earns a significant amount more a month than the other, the division of debt may not be equal. Consider the difference in income and ability to pay the debt when dividing it.

Be aware that your lenders have a separate contract with you. They do not care how you decided to pay the balance. If you didn't change the person responsible for the debt or pay it off and close the account during the divorce, the lender might still seek payment from both spouses.

Here is suggested language to detail your division of marital debt. List each of the obligations as they appear in both financial statements.

The parties have the following joint debts:
(Lender and last four digits of the account number)
($___amount of debt)

(Lender and last four digits of the account number)
($ amount of debt)

(Lender and last four digits of the account number)
($ amount of debt)

(Petitioner's Name) shall be responsible for

Name each debt and the approximate amount

(Co-Petitioner's Name) shall be responsible for

Name each debt and the approximate amount

The parties shall cooperate and remove their respective names from each other's credit cards no later than (DATE).

OR

Parties agree to destroy all joint credit cards immediately and request individual cards to be issued respectively, to avoid future liability. In the event, either spouse fails or refuses to do so, the other may contact the credit card company and cancel the card with the instruction to issue an individual card to the non - complying spouse.

Except as expressly set forth herein, the parties have no additional marital debt.

Neither party shall create or attempt to create any debt in the name of or against the other. They shall not utilize or attempt to use the credit of the other for purposes of producing any debt.

Each party shall indemnify and hold the other harmless against all liability because of default in performance, any claim resulting from the other one of them, or failure to perform his or her obligations. This claim includes payment of reasonable attorneys' fees and costs incurred thereby and all additional fees incurred by such failure and default.

After you drafted the language that accurately details:

- How to divide your marital debt;
- Who is responsible for what payments to what creditors;
- When the deadlines for payment are due;
- What happens if the debt is not paid as you've agreed; and
- The waiver of responsibility for the spouse not paying the debt

---

You are ready to move on to Maintenance and determine if one spouse should receive spousal support, and what that looks like for you.

MAINTENANCE

Earlier I explained how to calculate maintenance. We talked about needing to determine property and debt division first. We discussed the presumptive guidelines and how you may be able to negotiate different amounts and lengths of time than a court would likely award.

When drafting maintenance provisions, there are some points to include in the language.

The statutory language the Court relies upon for Maintenance is found in *Colorado Revised Statute §14-10-114.*

1. Is either or both spouses waiving Maintenance?

In some divorces, both spouses are working, earning similar incomes, and would not qualify for Maintenance under Colorado law. In other situations, the couple decides on a property division that accounts for any Maintenance that would otherwise be considered.

Here is an example of the language used for the Waiver of Maintenance.

WAIVER OF MAINTENANCE

(NAME) understands that C.R.S. §14-10-114 contains an advisory guideline to determine maintenance, and (NAME) reviewed the same. The advisory guideline suggests a maintenance amount of $(AMOUNT) to be paid to (NAME) for (NUMBER) months.

The calculation determines the amount explained earlier in the book. The Court wants to know that you understand the amount you may or not be waiving Maintenance.

Understanding (her/his) right to ask the Court for spousal maintenance (NAME) waives any and all rights (she/he) may have against (NAME2) for maintenance or support, whether temporary or permanent. (NAME) knows and recognizes that this waiver is permanent and irrevocable and will forever relinquish any rights she may have thereto.

In making this waiver, (NAME) acknowledges that he/she may never return to this or any other court to seek maintenance no matter how her health or financial circumstances may have changed after the date of this Agreement.

Understanding that you are never able to come back to ask the Court for an award of Maintenance after you waive it is crucial.

The Court will ask you on the record if you understand that you are waiving maintenance and can never claim maintenance at a later date.

If you are not waiving Maintenance, then you need to decide if Maintenance will be **contractual** Maintenance or **modifiable** Maintenance.

Contractual Maintenance means you agree to pay or receive a specific amount of money for a certain amount of time. When you agree to the terms of maintenance to be contractual maintenance, you limit the court's ability to change the terms of payment.

The benefit of contractual maintenance is knowing that if your income increases after the divorce, it won't change how much you pay per month in maintenance if you are the one paying.

For the one receiving maintenance, the benefit is knowing if your financial situation changes for the better, you will still receive a set amount certain for a specific period.

Here is an example of the language to use for

CONTRACTUAL MAINTENANCE

MAINTENANCE PAID TO (NAME)

(NAME) understands that C.R.S. §14-10-114 contains an advisory guideline to determine maintenance, and (NAME) reviewed the same. The advisory guideline suggests a maintenance amount of $(AMOUNT) to be paid to (NAME) for (NUMBER) months.

(NAME2) shall pay (NAME) on or before the 5th day of each month. Payments shall be made directly to (NAME) through EFT/Written Check/Auto-deposit (choose one method and give the last four digits to account if auto-deposit).

Maintenance shall be contractual and non-modifiable as to the amount or duration unless death or re-marriage of (NAME) occurs.

(*note that some clients decide a life insurance policy is necessary to ensure payment of the contractual amount should a spouse die during the period of obligation. Other clients find it unfair to continue to pay a former spouse beyond the grave.)

The other option is <u>MODIFIABLE MAINTENANCE</u>

With modifiable maintenance, you agree to an amount that is fair and reasonable now but may be subject to change in the future. If you leave Maintenance to the judge's decision, the payments are modifiable.

The Court will maintain jurisdiction to change the amount of Maintenance paid later if necessary.

Here is an example of language for MODIFIABLE MAINTENANCE.

Both parties reviewed the presumptive guidelines. (NAME)'s monthly income is $(AMOUNT).

(NAME2) has a monthly gross income of $(AMOUNT). Based upon these incomes, the amount of maintenance to be paid pursuant to guidelines is $(AMOUNT) for (NUMBER) months.

(NAME2) shall pay (NAME) $(AMOUNT)/month as spousal maintenance through ____________ or until maintenance may be otherwise modified.

The award of maintenance is based only on current circumstances. The maintenance is modifiable and may change upon written agreement of the parties or further court order.

The Court shall retain jurisdiction for future modification of spousal support.

(NAME2)'s maintenance obligation shall terminate at the end of (NUMBER) months or upon (NAME)'s remarriage or the death of either party.

(NAME2) shall pay (NAME) on or before the 5th day of each month. Payments shall be made directly to (NAME) through EFT/Written Check/Auto-deposit (choose one method and give the last four digits to account if auto-deposit).

Maintenance is intended to offer financial support for basic necessities with consideration of the lifestyle afforded the less earning spouse during the marriage.

Maintenance is meant to help the lower wage earner gain education or employment that they may have sacrificed during the marriage.

If you both worked during the marriage, earn an amount similar to what you intend to make in the future, then maintenance may not be a reasonable request.

If the income you are earning now is more or less than you were typically making during the marriage, the argument for spousal support or maintenance may change.

If you have any doubt that your financial circumstances may change for better or worse, then do not commit to contractual maintenance. You must make the best decisions for the events as they exist today while divorcing.

The last financial matter to discuss in your Separation Agreement is your taxes. Some couples have significant tax debt coming into Divorce. Others are expecting refunds that may be considered marital property. Let's talk taxes.

TAXES

Your situation may call for specific tax language regarding debts or refunds.

The critical points to address are:

- Have you paid all known taxes throughout the marriage?
- How will you file if divorce is pending after the end of the year?
- What will you do if you find out in the future you owe or are owed a refund?
- If there is a tax debt that accrued during the marriage, will you be responsible equally, or will one party be responsible for the debt? If so, what will you do to indemnify the other spouse?

Your tax provisions may read like this:

> *If the parties are married through tax year 20XX, they shall file a married filing jointly 20XX Federal and State tax returns. The parties shall share equally any tax liability arising from the return and likewise shall share any refund equally, for tax year 20XX. Each party shall timely provide all required tax documents to the tax preparer.*
>
> *If the parties' marriage is dissolved in 20XX, then the parties shall file separate returns for tax year 20XX, and each shall be responsible for any and all of their respective tax liability.*
>
> *The Parties agree that during the years of their marriage through 20XX(last yr taxes filed during marriage), they have filed joint federal and state income tax returns. All known past due taxes*

have been paid and there is no threatened audit or notice of any tax deficiency for past returns filed by the parties, jointly. In the event of an audit, deficiency notice or refund for any year the parties filed a joint return, then the parties agree that any and all liabilities owed as a result of tax returns during the marriage through and any and all refunds shall be divided between the parties equally. If either party receives notice from any tax authority or entity concerning taxes that accrued during the years the parties were married, that party must immediately provide a copy of the said notice to the other party.

CHANGING HER NAME?

As the marriage ends, some women choose to have their maiden name restored. Others prefer to keep their married name, either because there are children involved or she has established a professional reputation or identity with the married name that she does not want to change.

If you are not sure whether you want to change your name or not, then keep it for now. There is a separate legal process to change it later if you choose.

If you want to change your name in the Separation Agreement, here is the language to use:

NAME'S CHANGE OF HER LAST NAME

1. (NAME)'s current name is "(LEGAL NAME)."

2. NAME requests that her name be legally changed to "NEW NAME DESIRED."

3. The desired name change is proper and not detrimental to the interests of any person or provisions to this agreement.

Your Contract is *almost* complete!

You've allocated the property, divided the accounts, shared the debt, and determined if maintenance is necessary.

You have concise yet detailed language, so everyone knows what is to happen and how long the time frame is to complete each agreement.

The following are some standard provisions to consider including at the end of your contract. While not specific to your Divorce necessarily, they are meant to cover some "what if" situations that may arise later.

MISCELLANEOUS PROVISIONS

BANKRUPTCY

Earlier, we discussed the fact that your creditors are not bound by the agreements you make with your spouse about who is responsible for the marital debts. Also, you may not discharge support orders through bankruptcy.

Because of this, consider including language about what will happen if either of you files for bankruptcy after the Divorce, having taken on marital debts.

Here's an example:

A. Non-Dischargeability of Domestic Support Obligation. The parties accept and acknowledge that all domestic support obligations are non-dischargeable under the Bankruptcy Abuse, Prevention and Consumer Protection Act of 2005 (11 U.S.C.§ 523(a)(5),(15)) and Colorado Revised Statutes section 13 -54-102(1) (u). If one party declares bankruptcy and any of that party's obligations outlined in this Separation Agreement are discharged, the District Court retains jurisdiction to reallocate property and debt division, as well as modify maintenance and child support based upon an unconscionable change of circumstances associated with the discharge. If either party must enforce the terms of this Separation Agreement either with the Colorado District Court or the US Bankruptcy Court, the declaring party shall be responsible for all of the enforcing party's attorney fees and costs.

This language explains that child support and Maintenance cannot be discharged, or excused, through bankruptcy. Should either of you file bankruptcy after the Divorce and attempt to have marital debts discharged, that would open a creditor up to pursuing payment by the other spouse, could be grounds for opening the Divorce case to reallocate property or money.

INDEMNIFICATION

Indemnification is the language that eliminates one spouse's responsibility and liability from those debts or assets taken on by the other after divorce.

Each party shall indemnify the other for any debt, obligation, duty, or liability assumed according to this Agreement. Each party shall hold the other harmless for any claim, action, or proceeding brought against the other because of the non-performance of the party assuming the responsibility.

This indemnity provision shall include the payment of reasonable attorney's fees and costs incurred in connection with the defense of any such claim, action, or proceeding as well as any losses sustained by the non-assuming party as a result of the failure of the assuming party to perform.

ATTORNEYS' FEES AND COURT COSTS

While you may have tried to handle the divorce on your own, there is no guarantee you won't need lawyers to enforce agreements later.

Some couples agree to take on their fees regardless. Others want language indicating that if the other party is not upholding the contract, and the other must hire lawyers to enforce the agreements, the spouse in the wrong must pay.

Here's an example:

Except as outlined in this agreement or by further order of the court, each party shall be solely responsible for payment of their respective attorneys' fees and costs herein. The respective party shall also be liable for any other professional fees and expenses incurred by them separately related to this Agreement and the proceeding to dissolve their marriage.

DISCLOSURES

It is important to state with no uncertain terms that you have both provided all your disclosures and are not hiding anything that would prevent the other spouse from making a clear and well-informed decision when signing the Separation Agreement. The failure to disclose assets, debts, or information during the Divorce could be grounds for re-opening the Divorce case later.

Here is an example:

The terms of this Separation Agreement are based upon complete disclosure of the assets and liabilities of each party. Each party completed his or her Affidavit of Financial Affairs. They each swear to the truthfulness of the information therein. Each party received and reviewed the sworn copy of the Affidavit of Financial Affairs of the other.

Furthermore, the Agreement is based upon information that has been shared formally between the parties. Each party understands the other relies upon the information as disclosed. Should any of the information shared between them prove to be fraudulent, or contain significant misstatements, misrepresentations of fact, or omissions, the aggrieved party has the right to return to this Court for amended orders pursuant to C.R.C.P. Rule 16.2.

GOVERNING LAW

Sometimes spouses decide to move out of state to start a new life once the divorce is final. Couples often agree that the state where they Divorce, shall maintain jurisdiction should there be a reason to re-open your case, modify the Orders, or otherwise enforce agreements made.

Here's an example:

The laws of the State of Colorado shall govern all parties' rights and obligations, the interpretation, and resolution of any disputes which may arise under this Separation Agreement. This includes any matters of construction or interpretation or enforcement of the terms hereof; however judicial forum adjudication thereof may occur.

DECREE AND COURT ORDER

This language details your intentions to have the Separation Agreement become an order of the Court and enforceable as a contract and Court Order.

With the Court's approval, the Separation Agreement shall be incorporated into any Decree of Dissolution of Marriage, which shall enter in the action referred to above.

Upon the incorporation into the Decree, this Agreement shall become enforceable as a Judicial Order and Judgment of the Court.

SEVERABILITY

There may be a provision in your Separation Agreement that could be determined invalid. Meaning, it can't be enforced. You certainly do not want the entire Agreement set aside or found to be unenforceable if one provision is wrong. Use the following language to protect the agreements made.

If any of the provisions in the Agreement is found to be invalid, illegal or unenforceable, such invalidity, illegality or unenforceability shall not affect the other terms of the Agreement. This Agreement shall be construed as if such invalid, illegal, or unenforceable provisions were not included. If the deletion of such provision or provisions would result in a material change, the term may then be subject to further negotiation.

BINDING EFFECT

Some of your agreements may affect others in your family or those in charge of your estate later. It is essential to put all on notice and agree that whatever you decide to in your Separation Agreement will apply to all others.

Here's how we do that:

The terms of this Agreement shall be binding upon the heirs, executors, administrators, representatives, legatees, devisees, assigns, and agents to the extent and in the way it is binding upon the parties.

ENTIRE AGREEMENT

Sometimes spouses make agreements or promises that are not in the contract. You want to make sure that everyone agrees that everything is in the contract.

If it isn't in writing, it doesn't exist!

Here's an example:

This Agreement sets forth the parties' entire agreement and understanding concerning the transactions contemplated in it and supersedes all prior agreements, arrangements, and understandings relating to the subject matter in it.

WAIVER OF BREACH OR DEFAULT

As time passes, spouses may forget agreements they made or change the way they do things without officially modifying the contract in writing. You may also not enforce something once but expect that the agreements are still enforceable later. When this happens, the two of you may be breaching the contract or waiving your right to enforce certain agreements made. Make it clear that you do not intend this action or non-action to mean you are rejecting the other agreements you've made.

No waiver of any breach or default under this Agreement is valid unless in writing, signed and dated by both parties. Any failure to enforce a provision is not a waiver of any subsequent breach or default of the same or similar nature.

Neither party may claim a breach of contract unless the party has given notice to the other party of such breach and offers a reasonable time for a cure.

MODIFICATION

It is crucial to agree on how you will change your contract if necessary in the future. Any time you modify your agreement put it in writing and file the amended or supplemented agreement with the Court so it may be enforced later if necessary.

Here's an example:

Except where expressly provided for by statute or herein, this Agreement shall not be modifiable by the Court, but shall be modified only by the parties, upon mutual written consent.

WHEN AGREEMENT TAKES EFFECT

Some couples want the Agreement to take effect upon signing. Others choose to wait until the Court approves the decree. Waiting until the court accepts your agreement and enters it as an order of the court is the safest time to agree your contract will take effect.

If you are anxious to divide accounts and intend to follow the contract as you detailed, the contract may take effect the day you sign it. The default is that the Agreement takes effect upon entry of the court orders.

Parties agree this Agreement shall become effective upon the entry of the Decree of Dissolution of Marriage.

UNDERSTANDING AND CERTIFICATION

It is imperative that your contract explicitly states that no one forced you into this Agreement. You are signing the Agreement voluntarily. You have read and understood everything in the Agreement.

All of your agreements are in the contract. You were honest and forthcoming with your financial disclosures.

Here is proposed language:

Each party expressly certifies as follows:

I understand that I have the right to proceed to trial. It is in my best interest to resolve this matter without litigation as provided by the terms of this Agreement. I am entering into this Agreement freely, voluntarily, and upon mature consideration, and not

because of any duress, pressure, or undue influence from any person or circumstance. I have had the opportunity to consult independently and privately with counsel of my choice concerning my legal rights and liabilities and the provisions of this Agreement.

I acknowledge and certify that I am relying upon the financial information and data furnished by the other. I believe that I have the information necessary to enter into these binding agreements. I have given separate due consideration to all of the provisions hereof, including those for the division of property and I took part in drafting this Agreement. I clearly understand and expressly agree to all the provisions in this Agreement.

I further acknowledge and certify that I believe this Agreement as a whole, and each of its provisions, are fair, equitable, and not unconscionable. This Agreement contains the entire understanding between the parties.

There are no representations, warranties, promises, covenants, or undertakings between the parties other than those expressly set forth herein.

This Agreement shall be binding upon and shall inure to the parties' benefit and the benefit of his or her respective heirs and personal representatives.

The parties request that the Court approve this Agreement and make it a Permanent Order of Court.

Now all that is left are the proper signature blocks. You will want to sign your contracts in front of a notary public. Below you will see how to set up your signature blocks as well as the notary blocks for their convenience.

They look like this:

____

NAME, *Date*

Subscribed and affirmed or sworn to before me in the County of
State of Colorado,
this *day of* *Month, Year*

My Commission Expires:

____

Notary Public

____

NAME, *Date*

Subscribed and affirmed or sworn to before me in the County of
State of Colorado ,
this *day of* *Month, Year.*

My Commission Expires:

____

Notary Public

You've done it!
You've drafted your
Separation agreement!

You are steps away from finalizing your divorce.

ENTRY OF DECREE

After 91 days pass since the filing of the joint Petition or the personal service of the divorce papers to your spouse or waiver of service by your spouse ;

After you successfully drafted and filed all the necessary documents;

The Court can enter the Divorce Decree. The Decree is the legal document that officially dissolves and ends your marriage.

Here are the necessary findings the Court will include in your Decree for Dissolution of Marriage.

The Court has jurisdiction over the parties by virtue of the Co-Petition for Dissolution of Marriage filed on (DATE).

Both parties were domiciled in Colorado for more than 91 days before filing the Petition.

Ninety-one days from the filing of the Co-Petition, when the Court acquired jurisdiction over the parties, elapsed on DATE.

The marriage between the parties is irretrievably broken.

The Separation Agreement between the parties is found to be fair and equitable and not unconscionable as to support, maintenance (spousal support), and division of property, and is incorporated herein.

The Court therefore orders:

The marriage is dissolved, and a Decree of Dissolution of Marriage enters today.

Each party shall perform the applicable provisions of the Separation Agreement.

The Separation Agreement filed on (DATE) is incorporated into this Decree.

Any Support Order entered will become part of this Decree.

Date:

____

District Court Judge/Magistrate

Here is your checklist of documents that must be filed with the court before you can be Divorced.

- Petition for Dissolution of Marriage
- Sworn Financial Statements of each party
- Certificate of Compliance for each party
- Separation Agreement
- Proposed Decree.
- If you did not file a Co-Petition, the party who did not file the Petition should also file a Response.

If you do not have minor children, you may also file an Affidavit on Non-Appearance for the Court to enter the Decree without an in-person hearing or court appearance.

MOVING ON TO YOUR NEW LIFE

Now what? Now that you have your Divorce documents filed, either have your Decree or just waiting for the Decree for Dissolution of Marriage, what happens next?

To leave a marriage and to begin a new life is to realize and think about so much.

Think about your role in the marriage you left.

Think about what you need to heal and be the person you want to be before involving others.

Think about the future you want and what it will take for you to realize the good ahead of you.

Think about everything you can do to make you happy.

The freedom may be scary and challenging, or it may be exciting and rejuvenating after Divorce. If there is one concept 20 years of practice in Family Law and six years post-divorce has taught me, it is not to take alone time, the me-time, the redo time for granted. Learn to appreciate solitude and spending time with yourself.

To move forward is to live in the present. Do your absolute best each day, appreciating the gift it is - no matter how difficult. Believe in yourself, not the one in the life you are leaving behind.

I wish you the absolute best in creating your new story and life. There is no doubt, this next chapter, you <u>can</u> Do It Yourself!

APPENDIX

Colorado Courts have on-line forms available to download as Word documents and edit as described throughout this book.

A Draft Separation Agreement is included next. Should you like assistance with drafting your documents or want to see the forms we use for our clients, email me at TeddiAnn@DivorceInColorado.com.

<table>
<tr><td>DISTRICT COURT, CITY & COUNTY of DENVER, COLORADO
1437 Bannock Street
Denver, CO 80401

In Re the Marriage of:

Petitioner: SALLY SMITH

and

CO-Petitioner: HARRY SMITH</td><td></td></tr>
<tr><td>PETITIONER:
Sally Smith
1234 Happy Street, Denver, Colorado 80202
303-333-1212
SallyS@SugarShack.com

CO-Petitioner:
Harry Smith
1234 Happy Street, Denver, Colorado 80202
303-777-1212
Harry@Hotmail.com</td><td>Case Number:
2020 DR 001

Division: X</td></tr>
<tr><td colspan="2">SEPARATION AGREEMENT</td></tr>
</table>

Sally Smith, Petitioner, and Harry Smith, Respondent, submit the following *Separation Agreement* regarding the settlement of their respective rights as to their property, debts, spousal maintenance, and attorney's fees. Its purposes are those authorized by C.R.S. § 14-0-101 et seq.

I. RECITALS

1. The *Petition for Dissolution of Marriage* was filed on April 1, 2019, in the Denver County District Court, State of Colorado. The parties are referred to by their first names for ease of clarification and understanding of this *Agreement*.

2. The parties were married on December 31, 2000, in Denver, Colorado. The parties separated on January 1, 2019.

3. The following minor children were born of the marriage:
Jane, date of birth May 1, 2003, and
John, date of birth June 1, 2005.

4. Sally is not pregnant.

5. Both parties were residents of the State of Colorado for at least 91 days prior to the filing of the Petition.

6. The marriage is irretrievably broken.

7. To avoid further litigation, the parties have agreed to the following decisions relating to the determination of maintenance, the division of marital assets, payment of marital debts, and attorney's fees. The parties request the agreements set forth herein be made a *Permanent Order* of the Court and that the Decree enter dissolving the marriage to one another.

Accordingly, in consideration of these recitals and the subsequent agreements expressed in this document and for other good and valuable consideration not specifically enumerated herein, the parties mutually agree as follows:

II. PROPERTY DIVISION

8. REAL ESTATE

A. The parties jointly own the marital home located at 1234 Happy Street, Denver, Colorado 80202. The home has a current value of approximately $550,000.00. There is approximately $250,000.00 of marital equity in the home.

B. Sally shall keep the marital home located at 1234 Happy Street, Denver. On or before December 30, 2019, Sally shall refinance the marital home into her name only.

C. Sally assumes all financial responsibility for the home located at 1234 Happy Street, Denver, Colorado 80202, including but not limited to the mortgage, insurance, maintenance, and utilities. Sally hereby indemnifies Harry of all financial responsibility or any other liability for the home known as 1234 Happy Street, Denver, Colorado 80202.

D. If Sally is unable to refinance the home by December 30, 2019, she shall choose a realtor, and the home shall be listed for a price of Sally's choice.

E. Sally may continue efforts to refinance the home up until the contract for sale is final. Sally's ability to refinance the home shall take priority to any purchaser so long as she is able to satisfy the partnership loan and the aforementioned joint debts.

F. If Sally must sell the home, the parties shall equally share the costs for the sale of the home, including, but not limited to realtor and listing fees, and any necessary repairs that must be completed before sale, and any taxes owed at the date of sale.

9. MOTOR VEHICLES

A. 2015 Lexus RX

1. Sally shall keep the 2015 Lexus RX with an estimated value of $38,000.00 as her sole and separate property. There is an outstanding loan of $40,000.00 for the 2015 Lexus RX. There is no marital equity in the property.

2. Sally assumes all financial responsibility for the 2015 Lexus RX, including but not limited to the loan payment, auto insurance, and car maintenance. Sally hereby indemnifies Harry of any and all financial responsibility or any other liability for the 2015 Lexus RX.

B. 2014 Toyota 4 Runner Sport

1. Harry shall keep the 2014 Toyota 4 Runner Sport as his sole and separate property. There is approximately $6,000 of marital equity in the 2014 Toyota 4 Runner Sport. Harry shall retain the equity in the 2014 Toyota 4 Runner Sport.

2. Harry assumes all financial responsibility for the 2014 Toyota 4 Runner Sport, including but not limited to auto insurance and car maintenance. Harry hereby indemnifies Sally of any and all financial responsibility or any other liability for the 2014 Toyota 4 Runner Sport.

10. CASH ON HAND, BANK, CHECKING AND SAVINGS ACCOUNTS

A. BANK ACCOUNTS

1. The parties have the following bank accounts:
   a. Wells Fargo Checking x1234;
   b. Chase Checking x0101;
   c. Wells Fargo Savings x6789.

2. The parties shall divide the bank accounts as follows:

   a. Sally shall keep the Wells Fargo Checking x1234 and Wells Fargo Savings account x6789 and the funds associated as her sole and separate property.

   b. Harry shall keep the Chase Checking x0101 and the funds associated as his sole and separate property.

3. The parties shall cooperate to remove the name of the other from any joint account allocated to them within seven (7) days of the entry of the Decree.

11. RETIREMENT AND INVESTMENT ACCOUNTS

A. The parties have the following Retirement and Investment accounts.

1. Wells Fargo 401k x2222 with an approximate value of $100,000.

   a. The Wells Fargo 401k x2222 account shall be allocated to Sally. The Wells Fargo 401k x2222 and all funds associated shall be the sole and separate property of Sally.

Harry waives any further claim to this account as marital property.

2. 401k x5555 with an approximate value of $100,000.

a. The Fidelity 401k x5555 account shall be allocated to Harry. The Fidelity 401k x5555 shall be the sole and separate property of Harry. Sally waives any further claim to this account as marital property.

b. If a Qualified Domestic Relations Order ("QDRO") is required to transfer Sally's share of the 401k x5555, the parties shall each be responsible for 50% of the cost to prepare the QDRO. The parties shall use a mutually agreed upon expert to prepare the QDRO.

3. Fidelity x6666 with an approximate value of $500.00.

a. The Fidelity x6666 account shall be allocated to Harry. The Fidelity x6666 account and all funds associated shall be the sole and separate property of Harry. Sally waives any further claim to this account as marital property.

12. **LIFE INSURANCE**

A. Sally has Term Life Insurance policies through Wells Fargo.

B. Harry has Term Life Insurance policies through AIG Benefit Solutions.

C. Upon entry of the Decree of Dissolution of Marriage, either party may cancel or change their policies as they so choose.

D. Each shall keep $250,000 in life insurance secured for purposes of child support obligations, naming the other parent as the beneficiary so long as the children are minors.

13. HOUSEHOLD GOODS, FURNISHINGS, AND PERSONAL ITEMS

A. The parties already divided all household and personal property to their mutual satisfaction.

B. Each party hereby indemnifies the other for any financial responsibility or liability associated with the personal property in their possession.

14. BUSINESS INTERESTS

A. Sally owns an on-line Sugar Shack candy business.

B. The parties stipulate to a marital value of $1,000.00.

C. Sally shall maintain her business as her sole and separate property.

D. Sally assumes all financial responsibility for her Sugar Shack business, including but not limited to payment, insurance, and debts. Sally hereby indemnifies Harry of any and all financial responsibility or liability for Sally's Sugar Shack.

E. Harry waives any further claim to the business as marital property.

15. MISCELLANEOUS ASSETS

A. The parties have the following miscellaneous assets:

1. Frequent Flyer Miles through United Airlines with approximately 25,000 miles;

2. Marriott Rewards Points with an approximate value of 20,000 points;

B. The parties shall divide the miscellaneous assets as follows:

1. The parties shall share the frequent flyer miles equally based on the amount at the date of the Decree.

2. The parties shall equally divide the cost to transfer the miles, including but not limited to the processing and transfer fees.

3. The parties shall divide the Marriott Rewards points equally based on the amount at the date of the Decree.

4. The parties shall equally divide the cost to transfer the rewards points, including but not limited to the processing and transfer fees.

C. Within thirty (30) days of signing this agreement, the parties shall execute the necessary documents and cooperate to complete the transfer of the above-named miscellaneous assets to the other party.

III. DISPOSITION OF DEBTS AND LIABILITIES

16. MARITAL DEBT

A. The parties have the following debts with approximate balances as of December 1, 2019.

1. Wells Fargo Visa x1234 with an approximate balance of $16,000.

2. Key Bank Loan x3333 with an approximate balance of $10,000;

3. Best Buy x1234 with an approximate balance of $500.00;

4. Capital One x4321 with an approximate balance of $3,500;

B. The following debts shall be paid from the equity in the marital home:

1. Wells Fargo Visa x1234 with an approximate balance of $16,000.

C. The parties shall divide the remaining debts as follows:

1. Sally shall be responsible for the following debts and shall hold Harry harmless from any liability now or in the future:

    a. Best Buy x1234 with an approximate balance of $500.00;

    b. Capital One x4321 with an approximate balance of $3,500;

2. Harry shall be responsible for the following debts and shall hold Sally harmless from any liability now or in the future:

   a. Key Bank Loan x3333 with an approximate balance of $10,000;

D. Each party hereby indemnifies the other of all financial responsibility or other liability for their respective debts allocated to them pursuant to this Agreement.

E. Each party shall remove the other from each account allocated to them within thirty (30) days of entry of the Decree.

MAINTENANCE

17. SALLY'S WAIVER OF MAINTENANCE

A. Sally understands that C.R.S. § 14-10-114 contains an advisory guideline to determine maintenance, and she has reviewed the same. The maintenance worksheet yields a guideline amount of $0.00 to be paid to Sally. Maintenance is not applicable in this case based on the parties' respective incomes.

B. Understanding her right to ask the Court for spousal maintenance, Sally waives any and all claims she may have against Harry for maintenance or support, whether temporary or permanent. Sally knows and recognizes that this waiver is permanent and irrevocable and will forever relinquish any rights she may have thereto. In making this waiver, Sally acknowledges that she may never return to this or any other court to seek maintenance no matter how her health or financial circumstances may have changed after the date of this Agreement.

18. HARRY'S WAIVER OF MAINTENANCE

A. Harry understands that C.R.S. § 14-10-114 contains an advisory guideline to determine maintenance, and he has reviewed the same. The maintenance worksheet yields a guideline amount of $0.00 to be paid to Harry. Maintenance is not applicable in this case based on the parties' respective incomes.

B. Understanding his right to ask the Court for spousal maintenance, Harry waives any and all rights he may have against Sally for maintenance or support, whether temporary or permanent. Harry knows and recognizes that this waiver is permanent and irrevocable and will forever relinquish any rights he may have thereto. In making this waiver, Harry acknowledges that he may never return to this or any other court to seek maintenance no matter how his health or financial circumstances may have changed after the date of this Agreement.

NAME CHANGE

19. SALLY'S CHANGE OF HER LAST NAME

A. Sally's current name is "Sally Sue Smith."

B. Sally requests that her name be changed to "Sally Sue Jones."

C. The desired name change is proper and not detrimental to the interests of any person or provisions to this agreement.

TAXES

20. During the marriage and for the 2018 tax year, the parties filed all Federal and State returns jointly as married.

21. The parties believe that they have duly paid all income or other taxes, No other tax deficiency proceeding is pending or threatened against them with respect to the returns, and no audit is pending for them, to the best of their knowledge, information, and belief. Nevertheless, if the state or federal income liability for any such years is hereafter adjusted, by audit or otherwise, any additional tax liability, including interest and penalties, or any refund, shall be borne or received (as applicable) by the party whose income or deductions caused the additional liability or refund. For deductions or income not traceable to either party, the parties agree to divide such liability or refund equally.

22. So long as the Decree enters before the end of 2019, the parties shall file taxes separately. If the parties are still married at the end of 2019, they shall file taxes as married filing separately. Should they confer with a CPA who advises them otherwise, the parties shall cooperate in filing taxes in a manner most beneficial for them.

MISCELLANEOUS PROVISIONS.

23. INDEMNIFICATION

Each party assumes financial obligations under this *Agreement*. Each party now indemnifies and holds the other harmless against all liability for any default in performance by the other. Should any claim arise against the non-assuming party because of a default, the other shall indemnify them entirely, including payment of attorneys' fees and costs, and any additional fees and costs incurred by the party who has assumed the financial obligation's failure or default.

24. ADVICE OF COUNSEL:

The parties state and agree that each has had the benefit of consultation or the opportunity to consult with his or her certified public accountant or other financial/tax expert in connection with this case, and each is satisfied that they understand their situation concerning taxes. The parties acknowledge that their respective attorneys are not tax experts. The parties should consult with and rely only on the advice of their certified public accountant or other financial advisor respecting the tax and financial planning analyses/aspects of this case, and that of the provisions of this agreement.

25. BANKRUPTCY

Non-Discharge ability of Domestic Support Obligation. The parties accept and acknowledge that all domestic support obligations are non-dischargeable under the Bankruptcy Abuse, Prevention and Consumer Protection Act of 2005 (11 U.S.C.§ 523(a) (5), (15)) and Colorado Revised Statutes section 13 -54-102(1) (u).

26. INDEMNIFICATION

1. Each party shall and does now indemnify the other for any debt, obligation, duty or liability assumed according to this *Agreement* by that party but not by the other. Each party shall hold the other harmless for any claim, action, or proceeding brought against the other because of the non-performance of the party assuming the responsibility.

2. This indemnity provision shall include the payment of reasonable attorney's fees and costs incurred in connection with the defense of any such claim, action, or proceeding as well as any losses sustained by the non-assuming party as the result of the failure of the assuming party to perform.

3. The parties specifically authorize the Court to order additional payments, transfer the title of assets from one of them to the other or make such other and further orders as may be just and equitable to indemnify and hold the innocent party harmless from the loss or liability.

27. ATTORNEYS' FEES AND COURT COSTS

Except as set forth in this agreement or by further order of the court, each party shall be solely and separately responsible for payment of their respective attorneys' fees and costs herein and any other professional fees and costs incurred by them separately related to this *Agreement* and the proceeding to dissolve their marriage.

28. DISCLOSURES

The parties agree that the terms agreed to in this *Separation Agreement* are based upon a full and complete disclosure by and between the parties of the assets and liabilities of each of the parties. Each has completed his or her *Affidavit of Financial Affairs* and has sworn to the truthfulness of the information contained therein, and each has been provided with a sworn copy of the *Affidavit of Financial Affairs* of the other. Furthermore, the within *Agreement* is based upon information that has been shared formally between the parties, in accordance with the Colorado Rules of Civil Procedure Rule 76. Each party is aware of the other's reliance upon all such information; each agrees that should any of the information shared between them prove to be fraudulent or to contain significant misstatements, misrepresentations of fact, or omissions, each understands that the aggrieved party shall have the right to return to this Court for amended orders concerning the affected provisions of this *Agreement* pursuant to C.R.C.P. Rule 16.2.

29. GOVERNING LAW

The laws of the State of Colorado shall govern all parties' rights and obligations hereunder and the interpretation and resolution of any disputes which may arise under this *Separation Agreement*, including any matters of construction or interpretation or enforcement of the terms hereof whenever, wherever and in whatever judicial forum adjudication thereof may be attempted or may arise.

30. DECREE AND COURT ORDER

This *Separation Agreement* shall be tendered to the Court, for Court approval. Upon the approval of the Court, the Agreement shall be incorporated into any *Decree of Dissolution of Marriage*. Upon such incorporation into the Decree, this *Agreement* shall become enforceable as a *Judicial Order* and *Judgment of the Court*.

31. SEVERABILITY

In the event that any one or more of the provisions contained herein shall, for any reason, be held to be invalid, illegal or unenforceable in any respect, such invalidity, illegality or unenforceability shall not affect any other provisions of this agreement, but this agreement shall be construed as if such invalid, illegal or unenforceable provisions had never been contained herein unless the deletion of such provision or provisions would result in such a material change to cause completion of the transactions contemplated herein to be unreasonable.

32. BINDING EFFECT

The terms of this *Agreement* shall be binding upon the heirs, executors, administrators, representatives, legatees, devisees, assigns, and agents to the extent and in the manner in which it is binding upon the parties.

33. ENTIRE AGREEMENT

This Agreement sets forth the parties' entire agreement and understanding with respect to the transactions contemplated in it and supersedes all prior agreements, arrangements, and understandings relating to the subject matter in it.

34. WAIVER OF BREACH OR DEFAULT

No waiver of any breach or default under this *Agreement* shall be considered valid unless in a writing that is signed and dated by both parties, and no such waiver shall be deemed a waiver of any subsequent breach or default of the same or similar nature. No breach of this *Agreement* shall be claimed by either party in a court proceeding unless the party intending to make such a claim has given notice to the other party of such breach and has offered a reasonable time for cure.

35. INTERPRETATION

The section and subsection headings contained in this *Agreement* are for reference purposes only and shall not define, limit, or prescribe the meaning or interpretation of the text of this *Agreement*. No provision of this *Agreement* shall be interpreted for or against either party because counsel for one party drafted the provision.

36. MODIFICATION

Except where specifically provided for by statute or herein, the parties hereby agree that this *Agreement* shall not be modifiable by the Court, but shall be modified only by the parties, upon mutual written consent.

37. WHEN AGREEMENT TAKES EFFECT

Unless otherwise stated in this Agreement, this *Agreement* shall become effective upon the entry of the Decree. All parties shall abide by the terms of this agreement.

UNDERSTANDING AND CERTIFICATION

Each party expressly certifies as follows:

A. I understand that I have the right to proceed with a trial of this entire matter. I have determined that it is in my best interest to settle all issues without trial, as detailed by the terms of this *Agreement*. I am entering into this *Agreement* freely, voluntarily, and upon mature consideration, and not because of any duress, pressure, or undue influence from any person or circumstance. I have had the opportunity to consult independently and privately with counsel of my choosing concerning my legal rights and liabilities and the provisions of this *Agreement*.

B. I acknowledge and certify that I am relying upon the financial information and data furnished by the other. I have ascertained and waived to my satisfaction all of the facts and circumstances likely to influence my judgment herein, as I obtained such legal advice as I may have desired or deemed necessary. My attorney has explained to me all of the provisions hereof, as well as answered all questions I have pertinent hereto, and I understand them to my satisfaction. I have given separate due consideration to all of the provisions hereof, including those for the division of property, and I took part in drafting this *Agreement* specifically or through my attorney. I clearly understand and expressly agree to all the provisions in this *Agreement*.

C. I further acknowledge and certify that I believe this *Agreement* as a whole, and each of its provisions are fair, equitable and not unconscionable; that this *Agreement* contains the entire understanding of an agreement between the parties; and that there are no representations, warranties, promises, covenants or undertakings between the parties other than those expressly set forth herein. This *Agreement* shall be binding upon and shall inure to the parties' benefit and the benefit of his or her respective heirs and personal representatives.

D. The parties request that the Court approve this *Agreement* and make it a *Permanent Order of Court.*

______________________________	______________________________
Sally Smith	Harry Smith
Petitioner	*Co-Petitioner*
Subscribed and affirmed or sworn to before me in the County of ______ State of _______, this ____ day of ___________________, 2019.	Subscribed and affirmed or sworn to before me in the County of _______ State of ________, this ____ day of ___________________, 2019.
My Commission Expires: _______	My Commission Expires: _______
________________________	________________________
Notary Public	Notary Public

DISCLOSURE

The Do It Yourself Guide to Divorce In Colorado is offered as general knowledge. While the author is a practicing attorney in Colorado, this Guide is not legal advice or representation. The DIY Guide is a way to offer very general information and guidance through drafting documents necessary to Divorce In Colorado.

Should you need further legal advice, you may contact our attorneys for a consultation or possible representation after a direct conversation and engagement in services.

Teddi Ann is a Family Law Attorney & Mediator with offices throughout the State of Colorado.

Appreciating the complexity of the law and concerned with how many people try to represent themselves through Divorce, only to need lawyers later, Teddi Ann found it necessary to offer her legal insight and experience through this

"Do It Yourself Guide to Divorce In Colorado."

Spending the past twenty years advising families through the difficulties of divorce & family law, and watching so many couples make regrettable and unnecessary mistakes while divorcing without any legal or financial advice, Teddi Ann wrote this book to offer the same direction and legal insight that she provides clients paying her thousands of dollars to represent them.

During her career in Family Law, Teddi Ann has represented parents and children in cases of abuse and neglect, with the State involved; represented clients in interstate custody and parental responsibility matters, mediated numerous successful resolutions, and counsels many clients with multi-million dollar marital estates to try to keep their "*family business*" private and out of court whenever possible.

You can find out more about Teddi Ann and her practice at DivorceInColorado.com and UnifiedDivorce.org. You may also follow her on Facebook @TellMeTeddiAnn, and Twitter and Instagram @TeddiAnnEsq.

Teddi Ann Barry P.C.

UNIFIED DIVORCE℠
One Family, One Lawyer, One Solution

Made in the USA
Middletown, DE
20 January 2020

83450958R00066